# Stormie Omartian

# Out of Darkness

**HARVEST HOUSE PUBLISHERS**
EUGENE, OREGON

All of the stories related in this book are true, but the names of certain persons mentioned have been changed in order to protect the privacy of the individuals involved. Each name that has been changed is marked by an asterisk following the name the first time it is mentioned.

All photographs in this book are the personal property of the author and may not be reproduced without written permission.

*Cover photo © by Michael Gomez*

*Cover by Left Coast Design, Portland, Oregon*

*Portions of this book previously published in* Stormie.

**OUT OF DARKNESS**
Copyright © 2015 by Stormie Omartian
Published by Harvest House Publishers
Eugene, Oregon 97402
www.harvesthousepublishers.com

Library of Congress Cataloging-in-Publication Data
Omartian, Stormie.
Out of darkness / Stormie Omartian.
    pages cm
Continues: Stormie. 1986.
ISBN 978-0-7369-6638-2 (pbk.)
ISBN 978-0-7369-5057-2 (hardcover)
ISBN 978-0-7369-5058-9 (eBook)
1. Omartian, Stormie. 2. Omartian, Stormie—Childhood and youth. 3. Abused children—United States—Biography. 4. Adult child abuse victims—United States—Biography. 5. Women drug addicts—United States—Biography. 6. Life change events—United States. 7. Spiritual healing—United States. 8. Christian authors—United States—Biography. 9. Christian biography—United States. 10. Women musicians—United States—Biography. I. Omartian, Stormie. Stormie. II. Title.
CT275.O54A3 2015
270.092—dc23
[B]
                                                    2015020231

**Printed in the United States of America**

16 17 18 19 20 21 22 23 / DP-CD / 10 9 8 7 6 5 4 3 2

## Special Thanks

To my husband, Michael Omartian, for his faithfulness to God and to me.

To Suzy, Susan, and Roz, my prayer partners of more than 30 years, for all of your labor in praying for me and my family. I'd pray that the blessings you have given me through your ongoing prayers would be heaped a hundredfold back upon you, but then again I don't want to limit God!

To my son, Christopher, and my daughter-in-law, Paige, and to my daughter, Amanda, and my son-in-law, Dallas, for your love and support. And to my granddaughter, Scarlett Grace, for bringing everlasting joy to me and my family. I love you all much more than mere words can ever express.

To Bob Hawkins, LaRae Weikert, Kim Moore, Terry Glaspey, and the staff at Harvest House Publishers for your constant support. Special thanks to L.Rae, T.Glass, and B.Hawk for all of those special times we spent together talking about the future and how to best serve God. Our more than 30-year relationship has been a source of great happiness and encouragement to me.

# Contents

*Dear Reader,*

For the first 30 years of my life, I believed no one had more emotional scars than I did. I know now that I was not alone. After I began writing books and went public with my personal story, people came out of the hidden places of their soul with similar stories of their own to tell me. All were heartbreaking. Some were horrifying. In fact, many stories were so shocking that it was difficult to even think about them. I had no idea that these suffering people even existed, let alone how great in number they were. I mistakenly thought I must be the only one.

You may wonder how I didn't know about the countless people who have suffered emotional brokenness due to things that happened to them or mistakes *they* made. It's because, at the time, these kinds of negative experiences weren't talked about. They were kept secret in the unfortunate tradition of feeling that people might not believe you, or they would blame *you* instead of your circumstances, or judge *you* for *your* suspected part in the situation. We were in the dark ages back then about emotional suffering. And though we are not quite yet in the age of enlightenment about this, it's far better now than it was.

Emotional damage doesn't all happen in childhood. People can experience a wonderful time growing up and still be scarred later in life by abusive people who inflict their own brand of cruelty on them, or by their own bad decisions, or through tragedies of one kind or another. Whatever the reason, people need to be brought out of the darkness of their life.

This is the story of my struggle to overcome the emotional damage of abuse in my childhood and the heartbreak of being a potential child-abuser. But you don't have to experience any of these things in order to relate to the miraculous restoration I experienced. No matter what pain, disappointment, or situation has placed you in a dark place in your life, there is a way to come into the light of healing and restoration.

It has never been my intention to blame anyone for what happened in my past. It's too easy to point out someone else's faults, because we all have them. And because no parent is perfect, it's cruel and unfair to hold them forever accountable for mistakes they have made. We have to let those things go and take responsibility for our lives now. We have to move on. It's my goal to point you, the reader, toward the source of all restoration and wholeness.

This is a true story, but some of the names have been changed to protect the privacy of people. When that occurs, following the first mention of that name, it will be followed by an asterisk (*).

I wrote about some of the things that happened during the first 35 years of my life in a book called *Stormie* that was published in 1986. I began the story at the major turning point in my life that started my climb out of darkness. I've decided to again start at the point of deep darkness I was living in, in order to fully explain what drove me to the point of recognizing my condition and finding help. The facts are what they are, and I cannot leave them out because they are crucial to the rest of the story. The following 37 years after that point to the present day is all new, much of which I have not spoken about publicly before. But I feel the entire story should be told in order to prove that once you recognize the darkness for what it is, it's possible to walk out of it and into the light for the rest of your life.

This book is about my life, but it is not so much about me as it is about living in darkness and finding true light. We have all been there in one way or another. Because of the overwhelming number of people who experienced similar or far worse emotional hurt than I did, and because so many have given up hope of ever being healed, I'm telling my story so that they, too, can find a way out of the darkness of their past and onto the path of healing and wholeness that awaits them. I desperately needed restoration and I found it. And not only that, I found transformation such as I never dreamed possible. If I can find it, anyone who wants that can find it too.

I have prayed continually that this book will bring the healing, liberation, restoration, transformation, and sense of high purpose God has for each one who reads it. To all who desire to receive all that, may God so bless you.

With much love,

*Stormie Omartian*

*That was the true Light which gives light
to every man coming into the world.*

**JOHN 1:9**

# 1

# Paralyzed by Evil

I never dreamed I would live this long. I thought I would die before my late-thirties. And I certainly never imagined I would write this book. I loved to write from the day I could hold a pencil. I wrote plays, stories, essays, song lyrics, and poems. There was something in me that made it impossible for me not to write.

Writing is like breathing for me. In fact, I feel suffocated if I don't have time to write something every day. Writing always brought freedom to my heart and soul, and peace to my tortured mind—even if only temporarily. I wrote in diaries and journals about things that happened to me and the negative emotions I struggled to overcome. Writing released me and kept me alive.

I tried as hard as I could to overcome my situation and rise out of it. I wondered, *Why can't I be like other people who have never had to struggle as I have?* I clearly remember the day in my mid-twenties that became a turning point in my life. It started with a terrible tragedy for other people that severely affected me.

That day I woke up late. It was 10:00 a.m. and sunlight blazed through cracks in the window shades. My head throbbed as I opened my eyes. The stifling air indicated that already the day was hot. Long into a California heat wave typical of August, my tiny, two-room apartment never cooled down much. There was no air-conditioning, and it was too dangerous to leave the windows open even a crack. I sat up on my single-sized daybed and then fell back onto my pillow. Exhausted from a fitful night's sleep, I was too groggy to get up.

I had found another rose on my front door handle when I arrived home around midnight. This made the tenth consecutive rose placed there every evening after dark. It was beginning to bother me. What at first appeared to be a flattering gesture by a secret admirer was now becoming creepy. Only someone with a sick mind would continue this odd ritual day after day without identifying himself. I had a longtime problem with insomnia anyway, and this wasn't helping.

I had worked late the night before taping another television segment of *The Glen Campbell Goodtime Hour*—one of the top shows at the time. Originally hired as one of Glen's four regular female singers who dance, I had begun acting in comedy skits as well. Working with different guest stars each week was always a challenge, especially when there never seemed to be enough rehearsal time and I suffered from chronic doubt about my abilities. Taping day before a live audience began before dawn and lasted into the evening. I had once been very excited about it, but lately all I felt was fear and exhaustion. It wasn't the production. Glen and all the people with him were the best. It was me.

I sat up again, slowly this time, and leaned across the bed to turn on the television. I wasn't much for watching TV because I was afraid it would make my mind irreversibly numb. However, this morning, in order to get my thoughts off the rose problem, I turned it on.

The screen was full of a news report detailing the grisly stabbing deaths of actress Sharon Tate and four others in Benedict Canyon during the night. That was not far from my apartment! I drove over that canyon and went by her street frequently. Horror gripped me as the details of what happened unfolded. I didn't know Sharon Tate and her friends personally, but I knew who they all were. The slaughter would horrify anyone, but what I began to feel was beyond horror. Fear was growing inside me to a paralyzing terror.

It was the knives. Sharon Tate was stabbed! I had always had an unreasonable fear of knives. For as long as I could remember, I had suffered from recurring nightmares in which I was stabbed repeatedly. The mere *thought* of knives made me deathly afraid—far beyond what would be considered normal.

My phone rang and temporarily broke the grip of fear that kept me riveted to the TV. "Did you hear about Sharon Tate and the others?" inquired a friend on the other end of the line. Many similar calls followed. No one could believe what had happened, nor could they even begin to understand why. There seemed to be no motive for the murders, which made them even more frightening.

That evening I went out to a restaurant with friends, and the murders were the total topic of conversation. We all agreed that the heat wave made people crazy, and that the flourishing psychedelic drug scene of the sixties had brought with it a kind of evil madness that pervaded everything. This was August 10, 1969.

When I returned to my apartment about 11:00, there it was—another rose draped across *my front door* handle. I shuddered with fear as I suddenly realized there was a pattern to this madness. The roses had started out as tiny buds. Gradually, they had gotten bigger each night. And now they were beginning to open. *What will happen,* I wondered, *when the roses are in full bloom?* I hurried into the apartment, bolted the door, and went to bed in terror.

The next morning I turned on the TV as soon as I was awake to see if there was further news about the Sharon Tate case. Desperate to understand what happened and why, my mind was filled with unanswered questions. Much to my horror, during the night there had been two more stabbing deaths. A husband and wife by the last name of LaBianca were butchered. The details matched those of the Sharon Tate murders, and the police suspected that the killers were the same people.

Fear spread like wildfire all over town. The rich put up security fences, installed burglar alarms, and purchased guard dogs. The rest of us bolted our doors and windows and didn't open them for anyone. I couldn't stand being alone, and my boyfriend, Rick*, was out of town. My apartment was too small to have people over, so I went out with friends again that night, as I desperately needed to be with someone.

When I returned to my apartment at around 2:00 a.m., there was another rose on the door handle. This one was beginning to blossom. I quickly threw it into the bushes, ran inside, and bolted the door.

As I dressed for bed, my mind sorted through the macabre details of the stabbing death of Sharon Tate. Here was a beautiful and wealthy young woman, nine months pregnant, living in a big house with burglar alarms and an electronic fence. She was totally protected and yet totally vulnerable. I knew that she, and the others murdered with her, were not the type of people to be involved in occult practices as was implied by certain news reports. They were also not the type of people you would ever think could end up murdered. If Sharon Tate could have the sanctity of her home invaded in that way, then what protection was there for me? And the knives—I couldn't even bear to think about the knives.

But something more was bothering me. Something about the *spirit* of what had gone on there that was way too familiar. It was like meeting someone you know you've met before, but you can't seem to place him.

I'd been heavily involved in the occult for years. It started with Ouija boards and horoscopes, and then I'd dived headlong into astral projection and séances to summon the dead. Numerology fascinated me so much that I considered changing my name when I learned that if the letters in your name added up to a certain number, you could become successful and fulfilled. However, I knew of a promising young actress who paid a numerologist to devise a new name for her. She changed her name legally, moved to New York City to begin her life of success, and was never heard from again. A numerologist sending me into obscurity was not what I had in mind, so I decided to go on to other things.

I took hypnotism classes, which were very popular in the entertainment industry. I frequently went into a trancelike state and told myself things I wanted to hear. "Stormie," I would say, "you are a beautiful, successful, and wonderful person. You can talk, sing, and act, and you are not afraid."

But as with all of the other things I had tried, whatever help I received was fleeting, and afterward I felt worse than before.

Next, I threw myself into a manmade religion—also very popular in that town—that believed there was no evil in the world except what existed in a person's mind. And if you could control your mind, you could control the amount of negative experiences you would have. I bought every book available on the subject and read each one thoroughly. I associated with other likeminded advocates, which wasn't hard to do because so many of the Hollywood show business people, especially actresses, were into it. It didn't work out for me because, no matter how I tried to think good thoughts, I could still see evil everywhere, and the fear, depression, anxiety, and panic in me grew worse.

I became involved in anything that told me I was worth something and that there could be a life without pain in my future. I frequently visited mediums, hoping they could give me good news. When they didn't, I was despairing. I rode an emotional roller coaster, and there was no balance to my life.

Devoting myself to Eastern religions, I began meditating daily. However, the God I searched for so diligently was distant and cold, and peace eluded me. Once, when I was in the middle of meditation, I opened my eyes to find that I was looking at my own body lying on the couch across the room. This was the out-of-body experience I had read about and wanted, but it didn't bring me the "oneness with the universe" I had been told would happen. Instead, it brought greater terror. The more involved I became, the more I saw strange things—odd beings and forms floating in front of my eyes. I didn't understand what was happening or why.

Despite the frightening aspects of the occult, I was irresistibly drawn to it. I knew there was a real spirit world because I'd seen it. And the books promised that by pursuing these methods I would find God and eternal peace. Why did it seem to have the opposite effect on me? Yet because I was desperate for anything that could possibly fill my emptiness inside, soothe the intense emotional pain I felt constantly, and quell the unreasonable fear that threatened to control my mind, I continued my search. There had to be an answer for me, and I was going to find it.

Something about my occult practices reminded me of the Sharon Tate murders. I felt I was a part of what happened even though I knew I wasn't. Remembering the old adage "You always recognize your own," I found the events all too familiar. Somehow, I was aligned. I could feel it. I feared that if I continued the path I was on, what happened to Sharon Tate could happen to me. Yet I felt powerless to stop it.

*I can't think about it anymore,* I thought to myself as I slipped into a thin summer nightgown and headed into the bathroom to wash my face. I flipped on the light switch and was startled by the sight of hundreds of large cockroaches scurrying everywhere on the tile floor. I had lived there for more than a year and had never seen a single one before. But I had also never come into the bathroom so late.

I dashed into the kitchen for a can of pesticide and sprayed the bathroom ruthlessly until every bug was dead. The thought of sleeping there with even one living cockroach drove me on. When there was no sign of life, I finally stopped. By then the smell of poison was deathly strong. In my tiny place I knew I couldn't stay in those fumes for long, yet at two o'clock in the morning it was too late to go anywhere else. I opened the bathroom window as wide as it would go to air out the room and the whole apartment.

Then I went to my closet right outside the bathroom and began to hang up the clothes I had tossed there. As I put the last garment in place, I heard a rustling of leaves through the open window. My apartment building was located in the Hollywood Hills and surrounded by trees and bushes. I would often hear small furry animals scampering about outside.

I held very still and listened for more sounds. The rustling came closer and sounded more like footsteps than small animals. They stopped directly under the window, and I heard something slide slowly up the wall. When I saw what I thought was a hand grab the top of the windowsill, I was terrified. Having no place to hide, I screamed with every bit of bodily strength I could muster and ran for the front door. Thoughts of Sharon Tate, the LaBiancas, and bloody knives raced through my mind.

The one-story apartments in the complex I lived in were situated on a hillside, and each one was isolated in a checkerboard effect with bushes and trees in between. For me to run to someone else's apartment would be risky, especially if no one was home. Once outside, I stopped screaming and hid in the thick bushes.

I hardly let myself breathe. My heart nearly pounded out of my chest. I stayed like that for what must have been close to a minute. Then I heard movement again, this time on the roof of the apartment closest to me. That apartment was situated above mine and nestled into the hillside so that a person could hop on the roof easily from the street above it. I peered through the bushes, and a man's form was coming cautiously over the roof. He held a flashlight and shone it to and fro on the ground just in front of me. In back of him I perceived another person. The glare of the flashlight made it difficult to see clearly, but it appeared that there were two men dressed in black. One man yelled in my direction.

"Is anyone down there?"

I was silent.

He shouted it again with more conviction. I held my breath.

The third time he yelled, he turned in such a way that I caught a glimpse of a gun in its holster and what looked like a policeman's hat. From the bushes I called, "Yes. I'm down here! Who are you?"

"We're the police. Come out where we can see you."

"Thank God!" I cried as I moved cautiously from my hiding place. "Someone tried to come in my bathroom window. I screamed and ran outside and hid here in the bushes."

"We heard the screams from our police car as we were patrolling the neighborhood. You stay right there. We'll check around back and see if we find anything."

I was filled with relief that they had providentially arrived with perfect timing, but I didn't want them to leave me alone. I hid in the bushes again as they conducted their search. It was only a minute or two before they came to my door and said, "Whoever it was is gone now. Your screams probably scared him away."

They escorted me back inside the apartment and searched it to make sure no one was there. The apartment was so tiny it took all of 30 seconds to check the kitchen, under the single bed in the main room, in the closet, and the shower. There was no place else to look. They could have just passed it off as nothing but a petty burglar, but I could tell that because of the Tate-LaBianca murders they were taking this event seriously. I desperately wanted them to stay because I was still afraid. Instead, I thanked them profusely, bid them good night, and locked the door and the bathroom window. After they were gone, I couldn't believe that in my fright I had forgotten to mention the roses to them.

I went to bed but tossed and turned. With every noise my body stiffened and my heart pounded. I could hardly breathe from the heat, and sleep eluded me.

The next day Rick called. He was back in town after a long tour with his band. We had sung together in the same group for a couple of years and then started dating. I told him about the events of the night before, as well as about the roses, and of course we talked about the Tate-LaBianca murders.

We went out that night, and on the way back home we drove over Benedict Canyon near Sharon Tate's house because it was a direct route from Beverly Hills to my apartment. The road was deserted and appeared unusually dark. Terror crept over my back, inside my chest, and up into my throat until I was nearly paralyzed with fright. The fear was so strong that if someone had touched me at that point, I'm sure my heart would have stopped. I tried desperately to pull myself together so Rick wouldn't notice what was going on inside me. Keeping up a good front was always a priority. I had to make sure no one would ever discover what an emotional mess I was.

He walked me up the long, winding stairs to my door, and there, draped over the handle, lay another rose. He picked it up. The beautiful red velvet petals were unfolding.

"Stormie!" A young woman's voice penetrated our intense silence. It was my friend Holly*, who lived a few apartments down the hill. She was just coming in with her boyfriend. I grabbed the rose and ran down the stairs. "Holly, look! Another rose! They keep getting bigger, and I'm afraid that whoever is leaving them might be planning to do something terrible."

She was concerned as well. This had seemingly started as a joke, and we had laughed over it just the week before. But now it wasn't funny anymore.

"I have an idea," she said. "Let's wait out in the bushes tomorrow night to see if we can discover who it is."

"Are you serious?" My voice betrayed my fear.

"Don't worry. He'll never notice us. We figure he comes around ten every evening, right? Let's meet here at nine." Rick and Holly's boyfriend agreed to watch with us.

When the time came, we positioned ourselves in four strategic places, hidden in the bushes outside of my apartment. In order to get to my front door, the rose man would have to go by one or all of us.

We waited.

No one came.

We were silent except for a brief exchange at about eleven concerning whether we should stop at midnight or continue on. We continued. Midnight came and went, and still no one showed up. Finally, we were tired and aching from staying cramped for so long and decided to call it quits.

Holly and her boyfriend went home. Rick walked me to my apartment, came in for something to drink, and then left around twelve thirty. I readied myself for bed, and then I went to the front door to make sure it was locked securely. As I opened the door to slam it tightly shut, a bright, beautiful rose, almost in full bloom, fell at my feet.

I gasped and my heart started to pound. Quickly, I slammed the door shut and locked it. My mind raced. Always before, the roses had come around ten and never after midnight. The only answer was that the rose man knew we were waiting in the bushes. He knew Rick was in my apartment. He knew when Rick left.

He had been watching me.

I quickly called Rick, who had just arrived home. Without giving him a chance to speak, I told him what happened. "Obviously, we were being watched," he stated. "Perhaps it's someone in the apartment complex."

I called Holly, and she suggested that the two of us go door-to-door in the morning, telling our neighbors about the roses and the near break-in, and asking questions. Maybe someone had seen or heard something.

The next morning we started knocking on doors. *No one* had heard the screaming of two nights before, even though two policemen driving by had heard it from inside their car. No one had seen anyone suspicious. But, yes, they would tell us if they did.

The last apartment we checked belonged to a large, dark-haired, mustached man named Leo*. He was in his mid-twenties and a would-be actor like nearly every other male in town. We had talked briefly on several occasions, and each time he had asked me to go out with him. I always assured him I was seeing someone and he always backed off. I tried to maintain a friendly but distant relationship with him because something about him was strange.

When we questioned Leo, he said he had heard the screaming. This was odd because other people who were home the night of the attempted break-in, and whose apartments were closer to mine, had *not* heard it. I was amazed that he'd heard me cry so desperately for help but didn't check to see what was wrong. I told him about the roses, and he said he had seen no one suspicious.

"I'm concerned," I said. "Anyone who would leave a rose on my door handle fourteen days in a row without identifying himself has got to be a weirdo with a sick mind."

The moment I said "weirdo with a sick mind," I saw Leo's eyes wince and his expression darken. It was ever so subtle and only for a moment, but his look was exactly what one would expect if I had said that about *him*. In that very instant, I knew it *was* him. I had wounded him with what I said, and now I was even more afraid. Politely, I thanked him and we left quickly.

I knew I had to get out of my apartment as soon as possible, so that afternoon I found another apartment over Laurel Canyon and into the valley away from the Hollywood Hills. I moved quietly and secretly early the next morning while it was still dark. Because I had few belongings, the move was easy. I left no forwarding address.

Afraid that the rose man would find out where I lived and follow me, my first few nights alone in the new apartment were filled with fright. The Tate-LaBianca murderers were still at large and, as far as I was concerned, so was he.

But nothing happened. The roses stopped. Only the fear remained.

# 2

# The Great Escape

I rushed past the guard at the entrance to the giant CBS building. Having seen me almost daily for years, he just waved me on through. After going up the elevator and down the hall to the enormous sound stage where *The Glen Campbell Goodtime Hour* was being filmed—right across from the large studio where *The Carol Burnett Show* was also being filmed—I practically collided with the director.

"Sorry I'm late, Jack," I apologized, as I had done countless times before.

"You're working yourself too hard, Stormie," he reprimanded in his stern but kind voice. He knew I was filming another local TV program on the three days away from *The Glen Campbell Goodtime Hour*, which meant no time off whatsoever. The look on his face questioned my sanity. He always showed a fatherly kindness toward me I so appreciated.

Unable to confess that I was too insecure to turn down any work, I joked, "They're hounding me, Jack. Dumb blondes are the rage this year, you know."

He gave me a hug and said, "Get to makeup quick. Cher is sick and can't do the skit with Glen. You're going to do it."

"What!" I exclaimed with surprise, sudden terror in my heart.

"You're exactly the same size, so her costume will fit," he assured me. "You are a quick study and will have no problem with the lines. Besides, you've watched them rehearsing, so you'll remember the blocking."

I was constantly amazed at Jack's faith in me. "What about my own skit with Glen?"

"You'll be able to do both. Cher's costume lady will help you with the fast changes. I'll send someone to run over your lines with you right after makeup."

I ran straight to the makeup room and collapsed in a chair in front of the head man. "I need a miracle, Ben. They're making me a star today, and you have to make me beautiful," I said, laughing.

Ben Nye and his father were experts at makeup—and very well known in the industry—so I didn't have to worry about what he was going to do. I closed my eyes and tried to breathe calmly and pull myself together. It was only eight in the morning, and already I was exhausted. In the months following the Sharon Tate murders, I had filled my life with work. Not only did I have two TV series a week, but I also crammed every spare hour with recording sessions and commercials. I was obsessed with working. It helped me minimize my deep feelings of inadequacy and my fear of being hungry and homeless, and it enabled me to keep a tighter rein on the depression and fear that always threatened to control my life.

Depression was something I dealt with daily. For most of my life, at least as far back as 13 years old, I awakened every morning to the thought, *Should I kill myself now or can I make it through another day?* When my alarm had sounded at five this morning, I lay frozen in bed, trying to decide what to do. *You have an important job to do today,* I had told myself. *You're doing a great skit with Glen Campbell. Rehearsal has gone well.*

*No, I can't kill myself today,* I'd finally decided. *If this part I'm doing turns out great, I might be recognized as an important talent. Then everyone will love me and I won't feel any more pain.* It had taken only a few minutes to get myself out of bed this morning; some days it took hours. Unfortunately, I believed I was only as good as my last performance, so when a job was over, so were my good feelings about myself and my life.

"You're gorgeous!" Ben said as he put the finishing touches of mascara on my false eyelashes.

"You're a genius, Ben." I smiled my thanks to him as I ran off to Cher's dressing room. It was the fancy one with the big star. The crew had taken down her name and put up mine in their own handwriting. It made me laugh, and I appreciated their constant support. I admired Cher, who was also in her early twenties at the time, and I thought she was one of the most beautiful stars I had ever seen. I was sorry she was sick, but I was also thrilled to fill in for her.

"Hi, Maggie," I said, greeting the costume lady.

"Stormie, we're late." She was concerned for me as well as herself. Jack ran a tight schedule, and wardrobe people were responsible for having the star dressed and in the proper place at the proper time. An aide came by with my lines, and Maggie helped me dress as I quickly studied them.

"All cast for the opening scene on stage immediately," boomed the assistant director over the loudspeaker just as Maggie zipped up the back of my costume. "It fits perfectly," she said, beaming.

I hurried to take my place in front of the camera on the mark designated by a little piece of blue tape on the floor.

Glen Campbell came in and gave me a big hug. "How're you doing this morning, lady?" he asked, smiling.

"Great!" I lied. "Do I look enough like Cher?" I nervously ran my hands through my long blond hair and blinked my blue eyes. Compared with Cher's dark-eyed, black-haired beauty, I felt terribly inadequate.

"You look sensational!" Glen stated in his usual sweet, encouraging manner. He was a wonderful employer, and besides admiring his talent, I adored him as a person.

"Cameras are rolling! Five, four, three, two, one...action!"

I remembered all of the blocking, and with the help of cue cards I got through all the lines without a mistake.

"Great!" boomed Jack's voice over the PA system. "Let's run it one more time, and I think we'll have it. Good job, Stormie. I knew you could do it!" I was elated to hear that encouragement and wondered why I myself could never feel that good about anything I did.

On my way back to the dressing room after the scene was over, one of the other singers said, "The costume looks great, Stormie. Too bad you don't have Cher's voice."

"Yes, and her money too," I replied, laughing to hide my hurt.

While perhaps the comment was spoken innocently, it triggered a memory from far back in my past. Unreasonable fear gripped my chest, and unbearable pain from deep within my gut rose up into my throat and made it difficult to speak. My breathing became labored, and I felt as though I were suffocating. I had to get to a bathroom, dressing room, or empty rehearsal hall as soon as possible.

"I'll be right back, Maggie," I said breathlessly as I ran past her into the female cast bathroom. "Just give me a few moments."

Once inside, I locked the door of the stall and braced myself against the wall. I tried hard to stifle the convulsive sobs that were just beneath the surface. The pain in my gut was so intense that I wanted to die. When I contained myself enough to return to work, I acted as if nothing happened. Keeping up a good front for others was a constant requirement for me.

"You okay, honey?"

"Sure, Maggie. Just a minor emergency," I said, trying to laugh it off.

I breathed a shaky sigh of relief. Once again, no one suspected anything about my anxiety attacks. Because of them I didn't allow relationships to get too close. How could I ever explain my actions to someone else when I didn't understand them myself? I assumed I had these attacks because I was strange—a misfit. If I let someone get near, they might figure that out, and I couldn't bear the thought of rejection. Besides, in my eyes everyone else was perfect, and I fell short by comparison. The closer I got to other people, the more intense the comparison became, and the more aware I was of all my shortcomings. It was better to remain at a distance.

After one more dress rehearsal, we went live to tape with a studio audience at about three in the afternoon. The taping day ended a success and I was relieved. "Great job, Stormie," a beaming Jack said as he left the sound booth to go home. "See you in a couple weeks."

"A couple weeks?" Then, before he could answer, I said, "Oh, of course. The two-week hiatus while Glen's out of town. Sure, see you then."

My heart sank. Because my other TV show had just ended its 13-week season, that meant no work at all for two weeks. The thought terrified me. When
I wasn't working, I lived in the throes of constant depression. I found that drugs
helped, and because it was the late 1960s, they were everywhere. In fact, they
were almost difficult to avoid. Psychedelic drugs were used commonly too, but
people were freaking out from them all the time, with some ending up in a
mental hospital. I wasn't about to drop any acid. I was too close to ending up in
a mental hospital as it was. And no cocaine. I had my standards. Simple marijuana was good enough for me.

I found that as long as I was either working or stoned I could survive life, but
I was extremely careful not to combine the two. I was way too professional to
do anything stupid, such as drinking or smoking pot. Work meant too much
to me to jeopardize it in any way.

That night I took some pills to help me sleep and went to bed dreading the
next day. As expected, I woke at midmorning thinking, *You're no good. Why
don't you kill yourself?*

*You did well yesterday, but yesterday is gone and you won't do anything good
again.*

*You'll never amount to anything.*

*Who are you kidding? Everyone knows you don't have it.*

*You're a nobody.*

Slowly and steadily depression sank on me like a thick, heavy blanket.
When I couldn't fight back the force of it any longer, I knew I was entering one
of my typical "blackouts."

For the next two weeks I could barely function. I lay in bed unable to read
or even watch TV, getting up to do only the minimum requirements for life.
The only thing that could have lifted the "blackout" was a call for work. But
no one called.

When *The Glen Campbell Goodtime Hour* resumed, I returned to CBS with
the usual mixed emotions. I was eager to work, yet always fearful that someone would find out about my lack of ability and my intense fear. I waved to the
guard at the gate. "Did you have a nice vacation, Stormie?" he yelled.

"Great!" I called back. "Not long enough, though."

"I know what you mean," he said, laughing. I laughed with him and perfectly masked the person I was.

As helpful as it always seemed, I recognized that marijuana was becoming a problem for me. One night before a trip to Las Vegas to work with Glen in the main showroom of the MGM Grand Hotel, I stayed up late getting stoned with friends. I slept a few hours and then left at 6:00 a.m. for the airport, not realizing I was still under the influence of the drugs from the night before. Traveling down the main boulevard to the freeway, I didn't hear an ambulance coming full speed in the opposite direction until it came over a hill. We were inches from a head-on collision. I jerked to the right as he swerved left. We were so close as he sped by that the air between us violently jostled my car. I braked to a stop to catch my breath, and I realized that everyone else on the road had already pulled to the side. They had heard the sirens; I hadn't heard a thing. I knew then that I was going to kill myself if I didn't back off from the drinking and drugs.

A few weeks later at Rick's house, I baked a pan of brownies with a large amount of marijuana he had mixed in the batter. Rick ate a few pieces, and I nearly finished off the rest of the pan by myself. I had an uncontrollable chocolate habit, and once I started eating it, I couldn't stop until it was gone.

It takes longer to get high from *eating* marijuana than smoking it, but once the high happens it doesn't wear off for a long time. I didn't pay attention to the amount I had eaten. At first I got giddy and silly, and then dizzy and numb. Suddenly, I realized I had eaten way too much because a crushing heaviness settled in my body and I felt as though I were going to pass out.

"I have to lie down," I said breathlessly to Rick as I stumbled to the couch and fell facedown. I hung on tightly to the cushion as the room began spinning so fast I thought I would disintegrate. Soon I couldn't move. I was paralyzed. My body felt dead, but inside I was still very much alive, trapped and unable to escape.

*Where is Rick? Why isn't he helping me?* I called his name. Or at least I thought I did. But there was no answer.

Six hours later I finally managed to lift my head. I could see Rick in the bedroom asleep. It took another two hours to force my body to the kitchen, where I washed my face with cold water and got something to drink.

*What a stupid move!* I'd almost killed myself again because of drugs. I knew I had to take action to correct my lifestyle or I was going to self-destruct, but I felt powerless to do it. Something inside was driving me to keep making bad choices—choices for death—over and over. I entertained suicidal thoughts every day, but it wasn't that I really wanted to die. It was just that I didn't see any other way out of the unbearable pain.

In the months that followed the Tate-LaBianca murders, the mystery surrounding them began to unfold. A group heavily involved in the occult and drugs was responsible. *I* was involved in the occult and drugs too. Was that where I was going to end up, with my mind so fried that I didn't even know right from wrong or life from death? Fear engulfed me more than ever now— fear of death, fear of rejection, fear of failure. I wished desperately that I didn't have to live alone.

One morning about four thirty, as I slept in my apartment, my bed began to shake violently, and a loud, overwhelming rumble from the bowels of the earth convinced me I was in the middle of a very bad earthquake. It shook more violently than any I'd ever experienced before. I thought the walls and ceiling were going to cave in under the weight of the apartment above me, and I would die a painful death—crushed, maimed, and all alone. The quake was violent enough to frighten anyone, and because my normal state was one of fear, this made me hysterical.

I ran for the door of my bedroom, but the force of the shaking threw me back and forth against the walls of the narrow hallway leading to the living room, where I landed hard against the coffee table.

I grabbed the phone and stumbled back to the hall doorway, where I knew I was safest. Falling to the floor, I tried to dial, but the tremors were so violent that my fingers couldn't even rest on the numbers. I tried three or four times before

I realized the phone was dead. The power was off in my place. There were no street lights outside either. In total darkness I dropped the phone, grabbed the doorjamb, and hung on tightly to keep from being thrown against the walls. "God, help me!" I pleaded. "God, please help me!" I had never been so terrified.

All around I could hear the crashing of my dishes falling out of the cupboards, paintings dropping off the walls, and lamps shattering against the floor. The enormous roar of the earth rumbled so loudly that I could barely hear my own screams.

What lasted only a few moments seemed like an eternity. Finally, the rumbling and shaking stopped. The sun was just beginning to rise, but I hung on to the doorpost until I could see enough to get to the bedroom, throw on jeans and a T-shirt, grab my purse, and get out. I didn't check the damage. That was the last thing that concerned me. Earthquakes that violent would have aftershocks that could bring the roof down. I was terrified of dying alone.

Once I was outside, I ran to my car and sped off as quickly as I could to Rick's house. Broken glass, debris, and fallen trees were everywhere. While I was driving, the first aftershock hit, and I pulled to a stop away from power lines to wait it out. The highway rolled and rippled as if it were made of soft rubber. Fissures in the road formed, and I had visions of the earth opening up and swallowing me so that I would never be heard from again. When it was over, I drove more cautiously.

On my way to Rick's place, I resolved that I would not live alone any longer. I wasn't brave enough to live openly with a man, and I couldn't live with a girlfriend because I desperately needed a man's affection. My steady stream of boyfriends would irritate even the most patient of women.

Marriage was the answer, and Rick was the most likely candidate. I had known him the longest of all the fellows I'd dated. We were somewhat compatible. Beyond eating together and having sex, what else was there to any relationship? Besides, he was one of the few men I was dating who was not married. I was forever ending up with some guy who had just freshly separated from his wife—or was intending to, as I would later find out. They weren't good candidates for the security in marriage I needed. Even if Rick wasn't the greatest choice for me, I decided I would rather have a two-year marriage with a nice friendly divorce than live alone.

Over the next few weeks I set about to manipulate Rick into asking me to marry him. I cajoled, pleaded, threatened, and sulked. I told him I didn't want to live alone, and we must either make plans to be married or the relationship was over. Finally one night he said, "Okay, I'll marry you. But it has to be 50-50 financially. I'll make a down payment on a house if you pay the mortgage and all the rest of the bills."

I told him that was fine with me. At that time I was making more money than he was anyway. Besides, I would have agreed to anything at that point.

After he put the down payment on the house we chose to live in, we made plans to get married right away. His family was Catholic, and although I had never heard him mention God in all of the years I had known him, he insisted on a Catholic wedding. What did I care? A Buddhist wedding would have been fine with me. I just wanted a male roommate.

A few weeks before the wedding, Terry, a young singer friend of mine, called to ask me to sing on a Christian recording session. She was the contractor for at least half of the studio sessions I did, and I'd also worked with her on many TV shows in the preceding years. It was three days of work, and I was eager to do it.

From the start, this recording session was peaceful and pleasant, in direct contrast to the stress and pressure of the Hollywood recording business. I didn't know any of the people in the studio except Terry, who informed me that everyone there was a Christian. She never mentioned the fact that I wasn't. She'd often talked to me about God and her church. And I thought that was nice— for *her*.

I watched each person carefully. Christians to me had always fallen into two categories. Either they were insensitive and obnoxious, trying to beat you over the head with their Bibles, or else they were bland, boring, uninteresting, and without any known personality.

The Christians on this recording session were different. In some ways they *were* boring because nobody drank, smoked, did drugs, or partied. I wondered what they did for excitement. Yet there was a very appealing quality about them. They were genuinely caring, and when I was around them I felt comforted and peaceful. They treated me like someone special, as opposed to the outsider I knew I was.

On our first break of the first day, Terry introduced me to a young man she had been telling me about for weeks. I gathered she thought we would be perfect for each other, so I was somewhat wary but curious at the same time. The minute I saw him, however, all doubts were dispelled. He was the cutest guy I'd ever seen. He had thick, dark, curly hair; beautiful olive skin; and large, expressive brown eyes that confirmed his Armenian heritage. He had an intensity about him and a sense of purpose that was very attractive to me. I was smitten the minute I saw him.

"Stormie, I want you to meet Michael Omartian," Terry said, and then she left us alone. Michael was warm and friendly, and I enjoyed his company immensely. As we talked I was transported to another realm, where no one else existed except us.

We were together every spare minute over the next few days, never running out of things to say. During one break, everyone except for Michael and me left the studio to go for coffee. He sat down at the piano to play, while I leaned across the side of it to watch his hands and listen intently.

When he finished the song, I said in amazement, "Michael, you're one of the greatest piano players I've ever heard."

He smiled, looked down at the keyboard, and shook his head. "That's nice of you, but it hasn't been easy finding work." I heard the frustrated musician in his voice.

"It's only a matter of time for you. You're a major talent, and it won't be long before other people recognize it." I'd been around Hollywood long enough to be certain that what I was telling him was true and not just flattery.

"It just depends on what the Lord wants."

"The Lord? What does the Lord have to do with it?"

"Do you know anything about Jesus, Stormie?"

"Sure. My Science of Mind books teach that He was a good man. Play me another one of your songs," I said, wanting to change the subject.

He complied, and I studied his intensity as he played. I was attracted to him in a profound way. He had a confidence and an energy I found irresistible. As my attraction for him increased, so did my confusion. *What am I doing?* I asked myself. I had no answers.

At the end of the third day, I invited Michael to my apartment for a health drink. He had been sick for weeks, he told me, and was unable to shake the congestion in his head. Having been into health foods for some time, I had a combination of things I knew would help.

"Hi, Michael." I smiled at him with enthusiasm as I opened the door to my home. I was eager to see him again.

"Hello," he said coolly. I was taken back by his sudden change from the warm and friendly person I'd met at the studio.

There was little conversation as I mixed up a concoction of brewer's yeast, wheat germ, lecithin granules, vitamin C, acidophilus, and more into a glass of grape juice. As he drank it, I could tell he thought it might kill him. However, my credibility was saved when 20 minutes later his head started to clear.

We made small talk quietly and with hesitation on his part. There was something different about him now. He'd been friendly at the studio, but now he was cold. I didn't understand it. Perhaps I'd misread his friendliness. Or maybe he felt uncomfortable about being in my apartment late at night. After all, he was one of those Christians. Or maybe he saw through me and found many things he didn't like.

When he left, I was painfully sad. I'd felt unusually good being with him at the studio, and yet this encounter had been strained. It reaffirmed my beliefs that there were no good relationships, only tolerable ones. You just had to grab a tolerable one and get all the life you could out of it until it was time to go on to the next one. I was getting married simply because I couldn't take living alone and Rick was the most tolerable of all the relationships in my life. We would do well if we could stand living together for two years.

Even though I accepted the fact that what seemed like a potentially fantastic relationship had fizzled, I couldn't get Michael Omartian out of my mind. There was a quality in him that I loved. Something beyond just physical, although that was certainly there too. I couldn't give it a name, but it was the same dynamic of life I'd recognized in my friend Terry.

Two weeks later she asked me to go with her to visit her friend Paul Johnson, a well-known Christian musician. Michael happened to be one of his two roommates. They lived up in the hills of Sherman Oaks in a beautiful, large, modern house with enormous windows that overlooked the city. The view was tremendous—and the view inside was even better with these three good-looking fellows. All of them had clean, healthy, vital good looks, plus that sweet, loving, irresistible quality I still couldn't put into words.

When I saw Michael again, he wasn't cold this time. Just tentative and cautious. As before, I was caught up somewhere between heaven and earth as we talked about one thing after another. He asked me out for dinner the following night, and I accepted.

At the restaurant our conversation began to move beyond things, places, and people to the deeper topic of feelings. He explained that the reason he turned suddenly cool at my apartment was because Terry had just revealed to him my plans to be married. He was confused and baffled. "Terry thinks you're making a big mistake, Stormie," he said emphatically, "and so do I."

"I know I'm making a mistake, but I can't do anything about it. The whole thing is set in motion and I can't stop it." I swallowed hard to fight back tears.

I couldn't tell him I was terrified to live alone, that I didn't deserve anything better, and that if any man were to find out what I was really like, he wouldn't want me. I believed there were no good relationships, at least not for me.

I saw Michael every night for the ten nights before my wedding. Rick never questioned where I was, and he never wanted to get together. He was at his mother's house. One night Michael came to my apartment to pick me up for dinner, and Rick dropped by for a few minutes. I introduced them. Rick left immediately and never at any time asked for any explanation about Michael. The incident was indicative of our nebulous relationship.

It was obvious that Rick and I had no basis for a marriage. We barely saw each other for the two weeks before the wedding. It was insane. I knew Michael thought I would call it off, but my life was out of control. It was spiraling downward at a horrifying rate, and I thought getting married would keep me from hitting rock bottom.

The night before the wedding, Michael and I saw each other to say goodbye. He picked me up at my apartment, and we went for a drive. I was so depressed I could hardly speak because I knew we would not see each other again.

"What are you doing, Stormie?" he asked, his voice tense with frustration. "You're marrying a man you don't love. Everyone thinks you're making a big mistake, and I *know* you're making a big mistake. You can stop this now, so why won't you call it off?"

"I can't, Michael!" I cried. "I know it doesn't make any sense, but I can't stop it." My fear and my intense emotional needs were making my decisions for me. The self-doubt and pain were greater than my ability to do what was sensible. But I didn't know how to explain that to him. It would never make sense.

He pulled to the side of the road, took my hand, and said, "You know I love you very much."

"I love you too," I said as I fell into his arms and began to cry. "I love you more than I've ever loved anybody."

"Then why won't you call this whole thing off?" His voice now betrayed anger.

"I can't," I said, sobbing. "I just can't."

It must have confused him terribly. No normal person would have behaved that way. No one was forcing me to get married. I was choosing this myself.

Weeks earlier, when Michael had briefly tried to talk to me about Jesus, I had wanted no part of it. I'd assumed it would mean intellectual suicide to identify with Christianity, and I just plain didn't want to hear about it. Now I wished I had listened more, but it was too late. Even though I found it difficult to let go of the purity and cleanness of our relationship, I knew I had to forget Michael and get on with the problem of survival. We said goodbye, and I went to bed and cried myself to sleep with the kind of tears that mourn a death.

The next morning I awoke with my usual depression and suicidal thoughts. The sense of futility was greater than ever. I was getting married. This was the only feasible alternative for my life, and it felt as if I were headed for hell.

I worked through the morning depression by convincing myself that this marriage would be better than living alone. For a moment I thought of Michael, but I knew that once he learned what I was really like, he would surely have rejected me. That would have been devastating. I had to settle for some amount of security and a reprieve from my intense loneliness and fear. I needed a place to belong, no matter what the conditions were.

In an unimpassioned state, I went through the motions as Rick and I were married. My descent into hell began immediately.

# 3

# Sinking Deeper

ick, would you please rinse the breakfast dishes for me? I'll wash them
when I get home tonight," I yelled as I was about to leave for my 8:00
a.m. appointment with my speech coach.

"That's not my job," he snapped.

"Well, what exactly *is* your job?" I insensitively retorted. "During the
last year and a half we've been married, you've worked exactly four days. At
least you could stop watching TV for an hour or stay away from your mother's house one evening and help me with some of this housework. I can't do
everything."

From the beginning I knew that Rick was unnaturally devoted to his mother
and loved her far more than he could ever love me. He wanted me to be like her,
and I did my best to imitate her many good qualities, but I could never measure up. He used criticism to try to mold me into an acceptable human being.
I didn't respond well to it, however, and withdrew.

"The insurance on the cars is due today," he admonished me, completely
ignoring all that I had just said about helping me with housework.

"Oh, no! That's more than six hundred dollars! Can't you pay half of it?" I
pleaded.

"That's not our agreement. I made the down payment for the house. You pay for everything else," he boldly reminded me.

It didn't take me long to see that our financial agreement was an unfair arrangement. I was paying far more than he was. But I *had* agreed to it, and apparently there was no turning back.

I went out and slammed the door. Through the window I could see Rick return to the TV, where he would spend the rest of the day while the dirty dishes sat on the counter. *It's obvious this marriage arrangement is not working out as I'd planned,* I thought as I drove to my speech coach.

Living with a male roommate was definitely not what I'd expected. My loneliness actually *increased* daily, along with my fear and self-doubt. I now felt that I had been better off single. At least then I only had to financially support and clean up after myself. With my busy schedule and Rick doing nothing at home to help, I was constantly angry with him. There was no communication between us, and although we had a sexual relationship, there was no affection or tenderness outside of that. I needed more from him than he could give, and I resented him for not being able to give it. Silently, I demanded that he love and adore me, but he couldn't. He had his own problems, his own depression, and I was so steeped in mine that I couldn't begin to understand his. I had no idea what he wanted out of our relationship, but I was sure he never found it.

As I drove along Benedict Canyon I passed Cielo Drive, the street where Sharon Tate had lived, in the house where she and her friends were murdered. I shuddered. Even in the daytime I was still afraid to drive there. But my speech coach's home was just a few houses down the canyon from there, so this was the most direct route from my house to hers.

"Hi, Gloria. Sorry I'm late," I mumbled as I walked past her into the warm, rustic living room typical of many canyon homes in Beverly Hills.

"You look very tired today, Stormie. And why are you mumbling?" she asked, voicing her displeasure.

"I *am* tired, and I just had a fight with Rick." I tried to speak slowly, remembering all she had taught me.

For years I had studied with different voice therapists to try and overcome a

speech impediment I'd had since childhood. Hours and hours of tedious, boring exercises resulted in what seemed like only minimal improvement month
after month. As a child I'd tried to hide the problem by either being quiet or
carefully rehearsing what I had to say. That's why acting appealed to me. I could
practice lines over and over, work them out with my speech coach, and then
say them clearly.

Gloria had helped me more than anyone else. Besides our regular speech
therapy two times a week, she was part of every acting role I received. On this
particular morning, she was going to help me speak my lines correctly for the
next comedy skit I was doing. The rehearsal for that was at the CBS studio at
ten.

"Slow down! You're talking too fast," she said as I started. "You're slurring
your words."

I tried again. "No! It's too nasal. Start over."

A minute later she interrupted again. "Stormie, you're retaining too much
tension in your throat. Practice these lines with a wine cork between your teeth."
I dutifully opened my mouth so she could place the cork. "Now speak from the
diaphragm, not the throat."

Over and over I rehearsed the lines. Changing incorrect speech habits had
to be far more difficult than learning how to speak correctly in the first place.
We worked for a solid hour, and by the end I was exhausted and starting to
shake. I knew that the depression and a growing bitterness toward Rick were
taking their toll on my body. I was frequently ill, and I felt ugly and old. I was
dying inside. All the choices I'd made for my life that I thought would save it
were killing me. At times I felt as if there were other beings living inside me and
I wasn't in control of them. Perhaps this was because of all the drugs I had taken
over the years, or maybe the dabbling in the occult practices that had brought
about the out-of-body experiences.

As I paid Gloria and left, she looked at me with that same expression I had
seen on so many people. It was an expression that seemed to say, *Stormie's such
a nice girl with so much potential. I wonder what her problem is.*

I drove over the canyon, left on Sunset Boulevard, and on to CBS, eager for work as always but afraid of it at the same time. Because of my unhappiness at home, I threw myself into work more than ever. *The Glen Campbell Goodtime Hour* was just beginning another season, and I had a great part on the very first segment. Besides that, I was still doing every possible record session, commercial, movie background date, or television program I could fit into my schedule. As more acting parts came my way, I lived to do them. CBS felt more like home to me than my own house on Benedict Canyon.

That night I arrived home from the CBS studio earlier than usual. Rick was, of course, watching TV. "I'm exhausted," I said and headed upstairs for a nap. "Wake me up at eight and I'll fix us some dinner."

I climbed into bed and pulled the covers up over my face to shut out the daylight. The next thing I remember was Rick pulling the blanket off my face. My eyes were open and staring at the top of the wall. He called my name but I saw and heard nothing.

When he reached down and shook me, I was startled to consciousness in a fit of hysteria as I realized what had just happened. It was as if my spirit had left my body and had gone to a place of extreme torment. For a moment I felt as if I had lost control over part of my being and might never get it back. It was frightening, and I sobbed uncontrollably.

Trying to calm me, Rick said, "I'll get you some water." He began to walk away.

"No, no! Don't leave me here alone!" I pleaded. "Please. I'll come with you."

He helped me downstairs and sat me on the two steps of the entryway leading into the sunken den. As I put my face in my hands and cried, I didn't see him leave to go into the kitchen. When I heard the sound of footsteps down the hall, I looked up to see a dark form coming toward me. It looked like my mother carrying a knife, and I feared she was going to kill me. "Help me! Someone help me!" I screamed with out-of-control hysteria.

Sensing that I was hallucinating, Rick grabbed me by the shoulder with one hand and shook me hard. "Stormie, it's me! Rick!" he yelled in my face.

I looked at him in total surprise. "Rick," I said, sobbing. I thought it was…" My voice stopped. Apparently, the glass of water he was carrying must have reflected light in a way that made it look like a knife. But I couldn't tell him…I had never told anyone about that. "I don't know what I thought it was," I mumbled as I began to shake.

After that experience, I was afraid to be alone even in the daytime. As for Rick, he never mentioned the incident again. Maybe he thought I was going crazy, or perhaps he was too passive to care. He never talked much about anything.

A few days later I began to develop painful sores in my mouth. I could hardly eat or swallow. When I finally consulted a doctor, he told me I had a severe vitamin B deficiency.

"I don't know what your lifestyle is, but you're under way too much stress."

"But I eat healthy food and I exercise," I protested.

"Healthful food and exercise are good, but they won't balance out against too much stress. You'd better see about resting more and working less. And get rid of whatever is causing you anxiety. You're only 28. That's much too young to be having these problems. The older you get, the more serious this will become. In the meantime, I'm going to give you shots of vitamin B three times a week until you're better."

That afternoon I went home and looked in the mirror. My face was deeply lined around the eyes, mouth, and forehead. My hair was dull and lifeless; it had been falling out for some time. My skin color was a yellowish gray. My body was chronically fatigued and my figure misshapen instead of toned. The pain inside me was unbearable. I felt old and washed up, and as far as I knew it was a permanent condition that could never be repaired. Age 24 was considered old for the business I was in. Terrified that people would find out I was over that, I became desperate to hide it. Knowing that some of the others I worked with were even older than *I* was, and they were lying about it too, didn't bring any comfort for me.

I sank into a depression that overtook all of the depressions I'd ever suffered before. Once again I thought seriously about suicide and planned it out in detail in my mind. I never talked with anyone about what was going on inside of me, but on a record date once again with my Christian friend, Terry, I shared about my out-of-body experience and how it frightened me. She advised me to speak the name of Jesus over and over when I got scared. "It will take the fear away," she told me.

I thought that was an odd piece of advice; nevertheless, at the first sign of incapacitating fear I did what she said. Much to my astonishment, the fear lifted right away. The name of Jesus had no particular meaning for me, but if it had some kind of special power, then why not use it? At least *this* time it helped me.

My emotional affliction was affecting my work. I began losing concentration, and my voice failed because of severe tension in my throat. One evening a friend who knew I was struggling called to give me the name of a psychologist. "Why don't you give him a call?" she suggested. "He helped me a lot, and I know he could do the same for you."

"Is this someone who will *talk* to me?" I questioned, remembering all the money I'd wasted on doctors who, I felt, needed more help than *I* did. "I'm not interested in any more psychologists who make me do all the talking and then sit there looking either bored or as if they think I'm crazy."

"This doctor talks. And he gives good advice."

With that assurance, and the hope that he might help me control my emotional pain and cope with depression, I made an appointment for the following week.

I found Dr. Foreman* to be a likeable, polite gentleman. He was a distinguished, middle-aged, gray-haired man who was five times more expensive than any other doctor I'd ever been to, but if he was going to be five times more personable, it would be well worth it. Right away he treated me as if I were an intelligent person and not insane. This impressed me so much that I was immediately put at ease. He motioned me to sit in the chair across the desk from him.

"What's been troubling you, young friend?" he said with a warm smile.

"I live in constant fear, Dr. Foreman. And I'm not even sure what exactly it is I'm afraid of. I'm surrounded by people, yet the loneliness I feel is unbearable. I suffer with debilitating depressions and anxiety attacks that make me feel as if I'm dying. I have emotional pain all the time, and I don't know what to do about it. I thought getting married would relieve some of this, but it has only made everything much worse."

I couldn't believe I was blurting out all of that information to this man, but I couldn't hold it in any longer. Dr. Foreman gave me an accepting laugh, leaned across the desk, and patted my hands reassuringly. "Don't look so worried," he said. "These sound like symptoms of something deep inside that you have probably hidden away. It's as if you were a child and you locked what you thought was a lion in the closet because he was big and he frightened you. Through the years as you grew up, you often thought about that lion and how scary he was. But if, as a full-grown adult, you were to go back to that closet and let out the lion, you would probably discover that he was actually only a small cat. He seemed large to you as a little girl, but he is nothing to be afraid of anymore. What we need to do is open a few doors from your past and let you see that what was once so frightening no longer poses any threat to you now."

It amazed me that he chose a closet analogy when I had not even told him about that part of my life yet.

With Dr. Foreman's calm, reassuring words, I knew I was finally going to tell someone my story—things I had never before told *anyone*. I took a deep breath and slowly began with my earliest recollection.

# 4

# Living in Darkness

I sat cross-legged on top of the large laundry basket that was filled to overflowing with dirty clothes. The musty smell of my dad's soiled shirts was comforting as I waited in the darkness of the small closet underneath the stairway. The old, two-story ranch house was so tiny I could hear exactly where my mother was most of the time. At that moment she was coming out of one of the bedrooms on the second floor, and I could hear her shoes on the hardwood as she came down the stairs.

I held my breath as she approached the closet.

*Maybe she's coming to let me out*, I thought. *Or am I going to get another spanking?*

Instead, she walked right past my door and into the kitchen. *I think she's forgotten me. How long will I have to be in here this time?* I wondered as I cried silently.

My only light source inside the cramped closet came from a small crack at the bottom of the door. I dared not get down from my position on the laundry basket to peek through it because of the mice and rats that frequently scurried across the floor. I was nearly four years old, and some seemed large to me. I was terrified that one would jump on me. One time I had found a large snake in

43

the small closet off the kitchen, and the possibility of another one joining me in this closet was very real to me. I made sure my feet never touched the floor.

*Why is Mother always angry at me?* I wondered in the silence. All I'd done was ask her for a glass of water, and she'd turned and yelled, "Get in the closet until I can stand to see your face!" I'd learned at an early age that if I cried or protested in any way, I was beaten and then put in the closet, so I never resisted. The force of my mother's personality was so strong that even my father seemed powerless against it, for he always let her do as she pleased.

I saw her shadow pass the door once more, and I could hear her talking to herself, or some invisible person, as she usually did. She had entered her dream world again, and it would be hours before Dad came home and she returned to reality.

I pictured Dad laboring outside in the hot sun. He was a tall, quiet, even-tempered man with a square jaw and large hands, who always worked long, hard hours just to eke out a living. When he wasn't working he was "dead tired," as he always phrased it. On that day he had gone to haul lumber for another rancher. Though he always had much work to do at home on our ranch, we needed extra money to make ends meet. I wished he were home more. Mother didn't make me stay in the closet when Dad was home. Once I tried to tell Dad about having to go into the closet, but Mother had called me a liar and I'd been spanked. I never tried that again.

Hot tears trickled down my face. I wondered if all children had to spend time in a small, dark closet. I didn't actually know any other children, for we lived on a small cattle ranch in Wyoming, about 18 miles from the nearest town and several miles from our closest neighbor. We had no telephone or television. Only the very wealthy had those, and we didn't even know anyone like that. So apart from the occasional visiting relatives, we were isolated from the rest of the world.

Visits by my aunts, uncles, and cousins were the highlight of my life. Mother was a different person when they came. She was cheerful and outgoing—at least to them. Her ice-blue eyes sparkled as she played the piano and sang while everyone gathered around to join in. I admired her beautiful voice and pretty smile. I had heard my mother's sisters say that her dark-haired beauty reminded them of actress Vivien Leigh in *Gone with the Wind*. I wished someday I could see that movie.

My mother's pretty, good-humored younger sister, Jean, whom I adored, visited most often—at least a couple times a year. When we were together I was very happy. But the day she left, all that happiness went out of my life. It was like a death. We hugged each other goodbye, but as soon as her car left the driveway I fought back tears as Mother began her typical stream of critical remarks. "Nothing but a bunch of leeches," she grumbled as she turned and marched into the house. "All they want is free food and lodging. They have no consideration for our lives." I knew that wasn't true. They were kind and generous. But I stayed silent. Dad made no reply and headed out to the barn. Within a day I knew I would probably be back in the closet.

One time my mother's dad came to live with us for a while. Pappy, as we called him, became my best friend, and life was good as long as he was around. Pappy and Mother argued continually, but she never laid a hand on me while he was present. I missed him terribly when he left. He was a welcome reprieve from my miserable life.

Mother had two distinct personalities, and it was the bad one that she reserved for me when we were alone. At those times she was critical, cold, mean, and unpredictable. Her bitter anger could flare up instantly, and she frightened me so much that I had frequent nightmares about her. When people were around, Mother was highly concerned about making a good impression on them. It was very important for her to appear perfect. In fact, she often said to me, "I am perfect. I have never done anything wrong."

By contrast, she often told me I was ugly, stupid, bad, and would never amount to anything.

When I realized I was a very unimportant and undesirable person, feelings of helplessness, hopelessness, futility, rejection, abandonment, sadness, fear, and self-hatred settled heavily on me. They were words too big for me to fully understand or verbalize, but they were genuine feelings I experienced every day.

The hours passed slowly on this muggy day in the closet. The still, stale air made me sleepy, and I dozed for a while. I awoke to hear Mother walk into the kitchen to start dinner. A few minutes later she opened the closet door and let me scramble out. I was grateful to be free. Dad arrived home shortly after that and collapsed on the couch, saying, "I'm dead tired tonight." He was not gruff, yet it was obvious he had no time for me. Physical affection and conversation were not part of our lives together.

I was terrified of the dark, and because there was no electricity on the ranch, there was no light at night that I could turn on. When I went to bed, it was pitch-black except for the kerosene lamp light I could see coming from the kitchen. I pulled the covers over my head and didn't move. There wasn't any plumbing either. I dreaded having to get up in the night to try and find the bed pot in my room for that purpose.

One night I awoke full of fear. I must have had a nightmare. I slipped out of bed and headed to the kitchen for a drink of water. Mother was still there, and I nearly collided with her as I entered. In terror I saw that she was clutching a large butcher knife. The upraised steel blade gleamed in the dim light. A sinister smile crossed her face as she stared at me with her cold, steel-blue eyes. As I backed away, she began to laugh. It became a wild, howling cackle as I tore back up the stairs to my room and crawled into my bed. It was awhile before I slipped into a fitful sleep.

I awoke just as dawn was beginning to break and thought of Mother poised with the knife as if she fully intended to stab me. The memory of that moment of terror never left my mind. I had repeated nightmares about my mother in the kitchen with the upraised knife, laughing at my fear.

Shortly before my sixth birthday we moved to a small farm 20 miles from town. Like the ranch, there were no modern conveniences. No indoor plumbing—only a foul-smelling outhouse. No running water or bathtub. No phone, radio, or television. There were electric lights, which was a great improvement, but no heating except for a potbellied stove in the tiny dining room. Life was hard there; nothing came easy. The bright spots were the many nice neighbors who lived within a few miles of the farm. They didn't stop by often, but when they did, Mother was cordial.

I wasn't locked in a closet anymore. Actually, the place was so tiny I don't think the two closets were large enough for me to even sit down in. But the farm could be a scary place with so many rattlesnakes. It's surprising I was never bit by one of them because they were often discovered close to me, coiled and ready to strike. They were creepy and awful and frightened me more than anything else.

That winter I had a sore throat that swelled painfully, to the point where I was unable to swallow food. Even drinking was unbearable. My nasal passages filled with a thick, rope-like material that the doctor pulled out with a special instrument. As with everything else in that small town, the hospital was overcrowded and didn't have a bed for me. We had to make the long trip to town every day through the snow so the doctor could give me a shot and pull the diseased, ropey material from my nose. The treatment was painful, but I endured it, hoping I would soon be well enough to eat again.

After a few weeks in this condition, the doctor became disturbed that I was losing weight and getting weaker. He decided to send a sample of the nasal material, along with blood and urine samples, to a special clinic to find out what was wrong. We drove home to wait for the results.

That night a blizzard hit, and for the next few days we were snowed in. As the storm worsened, Mother made a bed for me on a cot in the dining room next to the potbellied stove. Temperatures were well below zero, and because there was no indoor plumbing, I had to again go to the bathroom in a big metal pot that was kept near my cot.

It became so difficult for me to breathe and painful to swallow that I couldn't eat or drink hardly anything. I grew weaker and felt death would be a pleasant relief. In the midst of my misery, I sensed a concern in my mother that I had never seen before. Frequently, she tried to give me something to drink, but I could stand only two or three sips before the pain became too unbearable.

A week after the doctor took the tests we still had heard nothing. The snowstorm made it impossible to go to town. We had 14-foot-high snowdrifts, and no way to contact him. Dad spent most of the day trying to get hay to the livestock trapped in the frozen, snow-covered fields.

One afternoon there was a knock on our back door. I was too weak to care who it was or to recognize how unusual it was to have a visitor in such severe weather. My mother gasped as she opened the door. It was the doctor, with snow caked over his heavy coat, hat, boots, and gloves.

"I had to come immediately," he said as he removed his coat. "I drove as far as I could and then walked the last few miles. Your daughter could die at any time if she doesn't have this medicine."

*The doctor came all the way out here to save my life!* I thought to myself.

As he removed his overcoat and rolled up his sleeves, he told my mother that I had nasal diphtheria. After a quick examination, he plunged a needle into what little flesh I had left on my bottom. I hated needles, but I was already too weak and in too much pain to care.

I went to sleep after he left, and when I woke up hours later, I could see the sun was setting as it reflected through the bottles of cream soda—my favorite— on the dining room table. My throat was already much improved, and for the first time in many weeks I drank the cream soda and asked for something to eat.

Mother seemed overjoyed, and when Dad came home she welcomed him with the good news of what the doctor had done. Dad, in his usual quiet manner, didn't say much, but I could tell that his smile was a sign of great relief.

It was a slow recovery. I had lost so much weight that I was extremely thin and weak. Mother's kindness made me want to stay in bed even longer. There were no harsh words now. She often smiled, played the piano, and sang songs. It was as if this near tragedy had given her a new lease on life.

As the snow melted and we saw the first signs of spring, I thought that perhaps life would be different now. No longer would I experience Mother's anger and harshness. We would be a happy family all the time. Unfortunately, that hope was short lived. Gradually, she drifted back into her unseen world, where she talked constantly to the voices she heard in her head.

∞

It was a fairly warm morning, yet I ran to the roadside shivering at the prospect of another school day. The small van stopped in front of me and the door opened. When I hesitated, the driver, with a wave of his hand, said, "C'mon, we don't have all day." The first few times he had seemed sympathetic about my fears; now he only expressed irritation. I was one of many stops on the hour-long trip into town that we made every day.

I hurried aboard and slid onto the second seat behind the driver. I practically mashed myself against the window, hoping no one would notice me. As more students boarded, the noise level grew. Everyone seemed to know everyone else, and their lively talk frightened me. I sat motionless and stared out the window, hoping no one would see I was alive. I got my wish. No one did.

When the van finally parked in front of the school, I'd survived another trip without anyone speaking to me.

School was even more terrifying than the ride there. Because of my long illness, I hadn't gone to kindergarten but started first grade as the oldest and tallest person in my class. I didn't have nice clothes like the rest of the girls. They had beautiful, shiny hair; mine looked like tangled straw. My one safe haven was the classroom itself. I never uttered a sound unless spoken to, and I obeyed every command and rule. The work was not difficult for me. I studied hard, learned quickly, and got straight A's.

My problem was *outside* the classroom. I was terrified of the playground, where children ran around screaming, laughing, and playing games I didn't know how to play. I'd never been around children except for my cousins, who visited only once or twice a year. I didn't know how to relate to anyone my own age. During recesses I hid in the bushes at the edge of the playground and waited for the bell to ring. If a teacher found me and sent me back to the playground, I would get in the longest line for the swings, which was a legitimate place for me to be for a certain period of time. When I got up to the front of the line I ran off to find another long line. I didn't know how to swing or slide.

During my second week, as I again stood in line for the swing, one of the boys asked me, "Hey, skinny, what's your name?"

"Stormie," I mumbled.

"You're kidding!" he yelled. "Hey, everybody, listen to this! Her name is Stormie!"

Everyone laughed, and I felt my face turn a deep red. Then someone yelled, "Hey, Stormie, how'd you get such a stupid name?"

"That's easy," someone else added, "I'll bet she was born in a storm drain."

"Or maybe she's a storm trooper," said another.

I felt panic inside me as I struggled unsuccessfully to fight back tears. I breathed a shaky sigh of relief as the bell rang and everyone headed back to line up for class. An intense feeling of loneliness gripped me, and I wanted to disappear from the face of the earth. How I longed for a normal name like Mary Smith so I would never have to be teased again!

My dad had named me Stormie when I was born because not only had I been born in a storm, but he always said that when I cried I clouded up a long time before the rain (tears) came. Mother had wanted to name me Marilyn, but Dad said the name reminded him of someone he never liked. My name had never bothered me until I entered school, and then it seemed as though I never heard the end of it.

Another problem was my speech. I became aware that I didn't speak well from the reactions of the other children. I couldn't form words correctly, and I tripped on them. On the rare occasions when I took the initiative to speak to someone, either I spoke so softly that they didn't hear me and I felt rejected by their lack of response, or else I stumbled embarrassingly over the words.

"Stormie speaks funny," some of the children said, laughing.

I dreaded recess and lunch, times when I had to relate socially to other children. There were no teachers or other adults who noticed my plight or even attempted to help me.

Home life was no better than school. Most of the time Mother's behavior was erratic and volatile. She would become suddenly angry and violent, punishing me for unknown transgressions. Other times she could go for days acting as if I didn't exist. Nothing I did distracted her. At those times she lived in a fantasy world talking to imaginary people. Mostly they were people who had done her an injustice, and she told them off. I learned never to bother her at those times because she would turn on me violently.

One day I took Mother's fake pearl necklace from the small jewelry box in her bedroom so I could wear it for the school pictures. I kept it in my pocket until I got to school and then put it on in the bathroom. All the other girls had pretty dresses, but every day I wore the same red-checked shirt and navy-blue long pants. The pearls actually looked silly with that tomboy outfit, but I didn't realize it at the time. I just needed something to help me look nicer in the photo. I also wasn't clever enough to realize that I would be in trouble as soon as Mother saw the pictures. I was just desperate to be attractive in some way.

A few afternoons later, shortly after I arrived from school, Mother asked, "Have you seen my pearls?"

"No," I said, trying to mask my panic as I wondered where I had put them. I knew I had taken them off in the bus on the way home from school and put them in my pocket, but I had completely forgotten to return them to her jewelry box.

Grabbing my arm, she pulled me to the kitchen sink. "I'll teach you to lie to me," she threatened as she pushed a slimy bar of dirt-covered Lava soap into my mouth until I gagged. "I found my pearls in the pocket of your blue pants. You stay out of my things and don't you ever lie to me again." After she removed the soap, I had to stand for a while with that horrible burning sensation in my mouth before she allowed me to rinse it out.

Oddly enough, that punishment was never as bad a memory as being in the closet, because this time I was actually being punished for something I did wrong. When the photo of me wearing the pearls arrived from school sometime later, she only laughed and I was relieved.

Somehow I survived first grade. However, two months after I started second grade, Mother took me on a trip to visit my aunt—her older sister—who lived in Nebraska. I loved being there because Mother was nice to me around other people and my cousins were great company. The only problem was, as we all gradually realized, my mother didn't intend to return home. My dad later said that there had been no fight, not even a discussion that would lead him to suspect that she was leaving for good. I overheard her confide to my aunt that she thought my dad didn't love her and that farm life was too hard.

I entered school in that city, and it was even more terrifying than the one in Wyoming. These were city kids, not farm kids. They were better dressed, more self-assured, and more knowledgeable. They had a set of mannerisms and expressions that were foreign to me. It became painfully obvious that I didn't fit in.

At lunchtime we had to travel in pairs for about six blocks to the cafeteria, but I was always the odd person who walked alone. That embarrassed me to the point of immeasurable pain. I fought tears all the way.

My loneliness became so intense that one day after lunch, as I was standing on the playground waiting for the bell to ring, I became desperate for someone to play with. I decided to approach a group of five children who were standing around a small tree, piling snow on its branches. I joined in and tried to laugh like they were laughing. Suddenly the largest girl turned to me and said, "You don't belong here. Get out! Who asked you to play?" The other girls added, "Yeah, go away!"

The pain of their rejection penetrated like a knife. I turned and ran across the playground, blinded by the hot tears streaming from my eyes. I came to the edge, but I couldn't stop. I crossed the street and ran the short distance home to my aunt's house. Once inside, I ran up the stairs to my room, crawled into bed, pulled the covers over my head, and sobbed into my pillow. Mother and my aunt had gone shopping, and my uncle was asleep in his room with his hearing aid turned off, so no one knew I was there.

As I relived that horrible experience on the playground over and over in my mind, I wanted to die. Was there no one on earth who would give me the time of day? I wasn't hurting anybody. I just wanted someone to speak to me and acknowledge in some way that I existed.

When my mother and aunt returned and found me, I told them I was sick to my stomach and had to come home from school. I got away with that excuse for a few days, but then I was forced to go back. I felt so hurt, unloved, and lonely that I stopped trying.

At Christmas, Santa Claus came for my three young cousins but not for me. I was heartbroken as I watched them open all their presents. I was told that Santa didn't know where I was. I wondered how could he know whether I was bad or good and not know where I was. I decided he didn't care about me either.

After Christmas we suddenly left my aunt's house. I didn't find out until later that my aunt asked my mother to leave and go back to my dad. Everyone was under the impression that we were going home, but that wasn't my mother's plan. We went instead to my mother's Aunt Grace in another city. There I was enrolled in yet another school, and Mother immediately found a job.

Aunt Grace's home was a large, pleasant, old two-story house, with a big front porch surrounded by lilac trees that were in full bloom in the spring and smelled wonderful. Inside, the house was comfortable and clean, and Aunt Grace was always cooking something tasty in the kitchen. In spite of these nice living conditions, I missed my dad terribly. "When are we going back home?" I asked my mother once again.

"I don't know. Stop asking me."

At this yet another new school I resigned myself to loneliness. I made no attempt to embarrass myself by trying to be friendly and enduring cruel rejection. My only solace was reading books and writing letters to my dad. I simply endured the pain until school ended in June.

When Dad finally came to visit at the end of summer, Aunt Grace informed Mother that it was time to go home with her husband. Because there was nowhere else to run, she reluctantly returned with him to the farm. Mother was despondent and immediately became her ill-natured self. Still, I was glad to be home with Dad.

We weren't home for long when disaster struck. A severe winter blizzard killed much of my father's livestock. When he was finally able to ride out on horseback, he found nearly all of them dead and buried under enormous snow drifts. That was a tremendous loss for us, but it didn't stop there. The following spring he planted crops, but they were all destroyed by a series of violent hailstorms. The hardships of Wyoming farm life were no longer bearable, so my mother and father decided to find an easier life in Southern California. They packed up our few belongings and headed west for an unknown destination and perhaps a better life for us all.

# 5

# Terminal Hopelessness

The "better" life we left Wyoming for ended up being a small gas station in Compton that my dad leased, along with an old rundown shack of a house in back of it for us to live in. The front door of the house was four steps from the back door of the gas station, so grease and dirt became a way of life. An empty field adjacent to us was a breeding ground for rats, which had no problem finding their way into my bedroom. Occasionally, they were brave enough to climb up my bedspread and run across my bed. When that happened, I was paralyzed by fright and unable to sleep.

Dad worked fourteen hours a day, from seven in the morning until nine at night, six days a week. When he was not working, he was always "dead tired." Considering how hard he worked, we still barely survived.

Our poverty was obvious. No one lived in a worse house or drove a car that was older or more rundown than ours. And even though I was able to get five new dresses for school—one for every day of the week—they were of such poor quality that they soon looked dowdy, worn, and ill fitting. Yet they had to last the entire year, along with one cheap pair of shoes. They always fell apart about halfway through the year and had to be glued together. They were embarrassing.

We ate so poorly at home that my hot lunch at school seemed to me like the finest gourmet meal. I couldn't believe how the other kids joked about it and refused to eat the food. I went to bed hungry many nights when there was nothing in the kitchen but a nearly empty jar of mayonnaise and a bottle of ketchup. I usually lived on peanut-butter-and-jelly sandwiches. I was extremely grateful for the lunch at school and I ate every bit of it, no matter what it was.

Between the hunger, and the rats, and the poverty, life again seemed hopeless. My escape was to dream about being a beautiful movie star. I would make millions of dollars, wear beautiful clothes, be chauffeured in a limousine, and live in a palatial home kept spotless by a full-time housekeeper. Adoring fans would give me the love I had never known.

I had new hope and happiness when my sister was born. For a while she provided Mother with someone else to focus on besides me. And I was ecstatic. Though Suzy was nearly 12 years younger than I was, I viewed her as a companion—someone to talk to, to relate to, to love and hold. I saw her as my ticket out of intense loneliness. Also, seeing my mother care for someone else gave me hope that she really was human.

One afternoon when I arrived home from school, I could hear three-week-old Suzy crying in Mother's bedroom. I went into my own bedroom to attack a pile of homework, and suddenly Mother was standing over me. As I looked up, she dropped Suzy into my arms.

"Here! She's yours now."

"But I'm doing my homework," I protested.

"Don't argue with me. From now on Suzy is your responsibility. When you're not in school, you will take care of her."

"But I was going to try out for the play—"

"You come right home when school is out!" she yelled. "Do you understand?"

I felt overwhelmed. How was I going to keep up with my homework? And I had finally started to make some friends, but now I wouldn't have a spare moment to be with them. I could never bring anyone home because the house was too filthy to have someone see it. And Mother didn't want anyone in the house anyway. I tried to resent Suzy for being such a burden to me, but I couldn't. Her sweet and loveable nature was very winsome, and I adored her.

One morning shortly after my twelfth birthday, I woke up with a throbbing headache. I could barely stand up straight because of cramps and back pain. I stumbled into the bathroom to show my mother the blood on my nightgown.

"Well, now you have the curse of all women," Mother said in disgust, as if what happened was my fault. She had never, of course, warned me about the changes that would occur in my body. For some unimaginable reason no one talked about anything remotely reproductive in those days.

As my breasts began to grow, I noticed that the other girls in school were wearing pretty little bras. Tentatively I asked Mother to let me buy one too.

"We don't have money to waste on you!" she snapped. She went to her bedroom, came back a few minutes later, and threw her maternity nursing bra at me.

"There. You've got your bra. Now get out of my sight."

"I can't wear this!"

"And why not? It was good enough for me."

"But it's way too big. Can't I buy my own bra? Please, I'll earn the money myself."

"No, you can't. I didn't have nice things when I was a kid. Why should you?"

That was her standard answer to anything I ever expressed needing, and there was no further discussion. So I had to wear what she gave me. I was mortified in gym class when I had to undress in front of the other girls. I tried to hide as much as I could, but was quickly discovered. "Where'd you get that thing?" said one girl with a loud voice. "Nobody wears that." I wanted to crawl into my locker and disappear as all the girls started laughing.

True to my mother's erratic nature, she shocked me one Sunday morning by saying, "Get dressed. We're going to church."

"Church?" I expressed my shock. We had never been in a church, outside of one wedding and two funerals that I could remember, except for the times my aunt took us when we stayed at her house. *Where on earth did she get the idea to go to church?* I wondered. It seemed like such an uncharacteristically normal thing to do that I was eager to go.

I got Suzy ready and we drove to a pretty little church not far away. Mother listened intently to the sermon and must have liked what she heard because we came back the next Sunday. A few weeks later, Mother started teaching a Sunday school class—an even more remarkably normal thing to do.

One great thing about church was that the youth group had terrific beach parties and picnics. I fell in love with nearly every boy in the group. They were nice and kind and fun, and I tried to attract their attention.

Unfortunately, someone caught me kissing a boy in the church parking lot while a youth party was going on inside the fellowship hall. Whoever reported it called the pastor, and he called my mother. "You've been out whoring," she yelled as she grabbed my hair, slammed my head against a wall, and began slapping my face with her free hand. "The pastor wants to see you. We're going down there right now, and maybe he will pound some sense into you."

I felt terribly ashamed as I was brought into the pastor's office. Mother had so frequently referred to me as a whore and a slut that now I felt like one as I stood before him. *He must surely be angry*, I thought.

But the pastor looked at me with eyes of compassion and love. He invited me to sit down and gently said, "I don't want a nice girl like you getting into trouble. I'm going to pray with you that this doesn't happen again."

*That's it?* I marveled to myself. He said nothing more except a short prayer. I was shocked. No beating? No punishment? How could that be? He treated me with respect and love, and I felt that I was given a second chance. I vowed to never forget his mercy and never violate the rules again—at least not around the church.

Before I started eighth grade, we moved to a relatively decent house in a lower-middle-class neighborhood of another Southern California suburb. Mother always improved during the first few months after a move. It was like a new beginning for her, and she tried really hard to still go to the little church. But it was a lot farther away now, and she just couldn't keep it up. She became irritable and mean again and started calling me shockingly obscene names, even worse than before. Corporal punishment was her sole mode of dealing with me. The only physical contact I had with her was when she slapped me across the mouth or struck my head.

Soon she was sleeping most of the day and roaming the house at night, carrying on conversations with invisible people. One night in a fit of rage—I have no idea what prompted it—she took the big family Bible she had bought after joining the church and hurled it out the back door, across the patio, and into a plot of dirt. I gathered she was mad at God and the church. She apparently forgave God, because in a few days the Bible was back inside the house. However, she didn't forgive the church and we never went back.

She made friends with a few of the neighbors on our street, and while she never became so normal as to have them over, she was at least cordial. But when they were not around she screamed and raged at me for no apparent reason. Her vocabulary became liberally sprinkled with the most disgusting profanity. She only referred to me in filthy names, the nicest of which were "whore" and "slut." Most of them I would never repeat to anyone. My little sister was learning to talk well, and she began to pick up some of the filthy words that Mother used and to treat her dolls the way Mother treated me. Mother was horrified. Fearing her neighbors would notice Suzy talking and acting like that, she carefully cleaned up her language and controlled her actions better—at least in front of Suzy.

Her discipline was consistently inconsistent. She became furious if I tried to clean our house, yelling, "This is my house, not yours! If I want it clean, I'll do it myself." Yet when I did something seriously wrong, like the time a friend and I took the car out for a drive before either of us had a driver's license, she did nothing. When I set my bedroom curtains on fire while smoking and throwing a match that wasn't fully extinguished into the trash can next to the curtains, she had no comment. It was though it never happened. Her behavior made no sense, so I never knew what to expect. Her constant degrading verbal abuse built such a deep hatred inside me that I sometimes wished she were dead.

Of course, I still couldn't bring anyone home from school. I never knew from moment to moment what condition Mother would be in. I was always aware of the fact that I lived in a crazy house—not like the homes of normal people. There was no laughter, no fun, no peace in our lives, and no hope for it ever being different.

I seldom saw my father. He left for the gas station before I got up and often returned home after I'd gone to bed. As far as my sister, Mother had an obvious affection for her. In fact, she went to the opposite extreme. While I was treated with violence and hatred, Suzy was neglected and received no discipline whatever. Sometimes I wondered if Mother was trying to make up for the way she treated me by going in the opposite direction with Suzy. Despite the obvious discrepancy, I never felt jealous. I was glad that Mother could actually be nice to someone on a regular basis. Besides, Suzy was cute and affectionate, and I knew she loved me because I took good care of her. She was my tiny friend.

During my last year of junior high, I spent a night away from home with my girlfriend Martina Hammil*. Mother was very angry about my going, but I did it anyway. When Martina and her mother brought me back the following night, Mrs. Hammil joyfully told us the news that she was two months pregnant.

A week later, as I walked in the door of our house after school, Mother grabbed me by the hair. She slammed me against the kitchen door and began slapping me as she screamed, "You murderer! You murderer! You've killed an innocent child! I hope you're happy with yourself, you selfish _____!"

My mind raced. *What could I have done? Maybe I left the front door open, and Suzy got out and was hit by a car?* "I don't know what you're talking about!" I yelled back. "I didn't hurt anyone."

"You killed Mrs. Hammil's baby. It's your fault. You didn't listen to me. I hope you're satisfied, you murderer!"

"What baby? Mrs. Hammil doesn't have a baby."

"She lost her baby!" Mother screamed at the top of her lungs. "She had a miscarriage, and it's your fault because you made her pick you up and drive you home. That's why the baby's dead. You murderer!"

I pulled away, dashed into my room, slammed the door, and fell in a heap of sobs on my bed. "Oh, no! God, no!" I cried. "The baby's dead and it's all my fault. Everyone will hate me. No one will have anything to do with me anymore."

After a while I started to calm down and tried to think rationally. I had to call Martina. I had to know what she thought about all this. I opened the door and tiptoed toward the phone. Mother saw me. "Don't touch that phone. It's my phone, not yours."

The next day at school I asked Martina what happened to her mom. "Oh, nothing," she said casually. "Mom just started feeling sick, and she went to the hospital and the baby miscarried. She's all right."

"My mother says it was my fault," I said sheepishly. "She said when your mom drove over to pick me up that it injured her badly."

Martina laughed. "How silly! My mother had been driving all along. Your mother is nuts."

I laughed with her, but inside my heart hardened even more against my mother. *Never,* I determined, *will I let her devastate me like that again. She may beat me and try to destroy me verbally, but she will never penetrate the hatred I have for her. From now on I will look upon her as a crazy animal, never to be trusted.*

Mother attempted to make Christmas enjoyable that year, but it was an empty time for me. The season where all families were happily together only pointed up the loneliness I felt, and I ached for it all to end.

Mother surprised me on Christmas day by giving me a small green diary. She gave me a couple of other things too, but I felt that this was an unusually thoughtful gift, and I cherished it. I loved anything that had to do with writing. The diary would be a wonderful way to express my pent-up feelings. I was so anxious to begin writing in it on January first that I wasn't even disturbed when I lost one of the two keys that came with it.

As I began keeping a daily record of my thoughts and activities, I particularly made note of who noticed me enough to say something to me each day and who didn't. I was desperate for affirmation. At the same time, I was suspicious of people who paid attention to me, feeling that there must be something wrong with them. Because there was never any closeness, communication, or emotional contact in my family, I tried to meet those needs through boyfriends. When that didn't work, I fantasized in my diary. Though I continued to do well in school, that was not enough to sustain the emptiness, loneliness, and desperation I experienced. "Isn't there someone who can love me?" I used to cry at night to a distant god somewhere out in the universe.

Mother seemed to know everything I did as if she had hired detectives. What I *was* doing wrong seemed mild compared to her accusations, however. The degrading, filthy language she used to address me, and the slaps hard across my mouth and head that happened suddenly and for no apparent reason, became more unbearable. I began having nightmares again about her coming after me with a knife.

Soon she had me thinking that maybe it was *I* who was going crazy.

"Where is your white skirt?" she asked me one morning.

"In my closet. Where else would it be?" I retorted disrespectfully.

"It's not there. You've done something with it. You're giving your clothes away to your friends," she accused. Then she ranted on about my negligence.

I searched through Suzy's room, the laundry, and the pile of ironing, but I couldn't find it anywhere. I didn't consider looking in Mother's room, for she was very protective of her private property and I was never allowed to even enter her room, let alone look in her closet or drawers.

Late that afternoon, when I went into my closet for something, there was my white skirt hanging right in front.

"Here's my white skirt!" I yelled to my mother. "Did you put it here?"

"It was probably there all along. You're so blind," she said with authority. "You must be going crazy. Your mind is very sick. I think you're mentally ill."

Although these incidents were common and I suspected that she planned them, part of me wondered, *Am I going crazy?*

One evening I was across the street at a girlfriend's house watching her prepare for a date. She was two years older than I and very beautiful and popular with the boys—everything I desired to be but wasn't. As I compared myself to her, my depression became unbearable. By the time I left her house to return home, I was filled with pain and self-loathing. When I opened my front door, I met two angry stares. Dad said, "Where have you been? What have you been doing?"

Before I had a chance to answer, Mother's venom began to spew out. "You've been whoring around the neighborhood like a slut. You've been with…" and she began to list names of boys I liked.

I fled to my bedroom. *How did she know all those names and details?* I wondered. *Sure, I've been attracted to those boys, but I certainly never told them or ever mentioned them to anyone. Especially her. How could she have known my thoughts?*

Mother followed me into the bedroom to continue her accusations. She spit out her words between clenched teeth: "Your father and I have decided you can't go across the street anymore. You can't see your friends after school, and you can no longer use the phone." She couldn't threaten me with taking away my allowance because I didn't get one, or taking away my privileges because I didn't have any.

When she finally left the room, I didn't cry. It was as if I'd been returned to the closet and I was a little child again. Fear, terror, hopelessness, and futility flooded over me, and I could not withstand the magnitude of it. The voice in my head said, *It will never be any different.* If that was true, I couldn't bear to face another day.

I waited until the house was quiet and my mother and father were asleep, and then I slipped into the bathroom, opened up the cabinet, and proceeded to empty every medicine bottle and swallow every pill I could find. I swallowed one and a half bottles of aspirin, plus painkillers, sleeping pills, and a couple of prescription drugs. When I was done I went back to my room, put on a clean nightgown and robe, and laid down in my bed knowing I'd never wake up again. This wasn't a plan for getting attention or shocking people into caring. I just wanted to end the pain.

I fell soundly asleep.

When I opened my eyes again, I could not focus. The room was spinning, and I felt weak, dizzy, and sick to my stomach. I rolled over, noted the bright sunlight, and tried to focus on my clock. It was 1:00 p.m.

*What happened? What went wrong? Why am I still alive?* Gradually, I remembered. Sometime in the middle of the night, Mother had held me over the bathtub and forced me to drink some vile thing until I vomited.

I stumbled to the bathroom and locked the door. The empty bottles were in the trash. Most of what I had taken was aspirin. I looked at the other bottles. The sleeping pills and pain pills were old, from the time right after Suzy was born when Mother had trouble sleeping. Maybe they had lost their power. Obviously, they weren't enough to kill me. Just enough to make me very sick.

As I returned to bed, I reviewed all of Mother's accusations the night before. Where had she gotten that information? How did she know about those boys? Then it clicked. The diary! The lost key! Everything was in my diary, and she was using it to spy on me. Even my most private thoughts were subject to her scrutiny.

From behind my closed door I could hear the sound of Mother running the vacuum cleaner. Whenever something horrible happened, she ran the vacuum. It was her way of denying the problem and appearing to be perfect. And what was the problem exactly? Was it me?

Or could it be that *she* was the problem?

I had seen enough families close-up now to realize that my mother was not normal. Something was terribly wrong with her. Lately, she had started talking about people watching her through the TV or following her when she left the house. When Dad or I had tried to dissuade her, she became hysterical, and the force of her hysteria overwhelmed us. The number of people trying to "kill" her was constantly increasing—Communists, Catholics, blacks, whites, Hispanics, the rich, the poor, Baptists, Armenians, the Kennedys, and on and on until the list eventually included everyone we knew.

When I finally got up late that afternoon, Mother didn't say a word, not even to acknowledge my presence or find out how I was feeling. And I said nothing to her. It was as if we had silently agreed to never mention this incident to anyone.

Two days later I returned to school. "Flu" was the explanation on the note from home. I wasn't sure why I was alive, but the crisis was over and for some reason I didn't feel like dying anymore. Maybe it was because I knew Mother realized she had gone beyond the bounds of decency. However, I entertained no hope that she would ever change. Telling Dad was out of the question. I knew that if I ever mentioned anything to him, Mother would accuse me of lying and I would get punished. He always believed her.

Mother, of course, still didn't extend herself to me in any way, but she stopped going for the throat. We went back to doing what our whole family did best—pretending that nothing was wrong. The only solution for my life was to finish high school and then leave home as quickly as possible. All of my activities from then on became geared toward that goal.

# 6

# Failure to Commit

My plan to escape from home had several elements to it.

First of all, after we moved again just before my junior year in high school, I revised my ways of gaining attention at this new school. I worked hard to emulate the qualities I saw in the people I admired and knew were going places.

I maintained good grades, having nearly always been a straight-A student. Once I got a B in physical education in eighth grade. When I showed my favorite teacher all the A's, he said kindly, "You should have gotten an A in PE too." I couldn't tell him about the suicide attempt and being sickly afterward, and that I didn't like getting into gym shorts because people teased me about being so skinny. I simply said, "I don't like PE."

"If you want to succeed in life, Stormie, which you certainly can, you have to do things you don't like."

I never forgot that. And I acted upon that advice.

I knew one thing I didn't like, and that was speech exercises. I found a speech book in the library and thought the boredom of it would kill me, but I knew I wouldn't get anywhere without professional speech therapy. So as soon as I turned 16, I started working in a department store in order to earn enough money to buy a car and pay for speech and voice lessons.

When I had saved $200, I told Dad about wanting to buy a car and asked him to help me find a good one. One day he said he'd seen an ad for a 1949 Ford for exactly that amount. "Let's go check it out." I was thrilled with Dad's interest. He could relate to me well when it came to cars. We always drove the oldest car that could still run, and he understood how to fix it up and keep it going.

The car wasn't much to look at, but Dad said it had a good engine, and with a few minor adjustments at his gas station it would be in great running condition. So I bought it and drove it home.

"What color do you want to paint it?" Dad asked.

"Blue. But I can't afford it right now."

"Isn't your birthday next week?" I couldn't believe what he was saying. But sure enough, on my birthday, Dad drove the car into the driveway. It was painted my favorite shade of blue. There had been a sale at a popular car painting place, and they did it for $24.99. It was perfect. I saw Mother watching us through the window as I gave Dad a big hug and took the car for a spin.

Mother glared at me when I arrived back home. "I didn't have a car when I was a teenager," she sneered. "Why should you have one? Think you're something special, don't you?" I silently walked past her to my room and slammed the door. Through the closed door she shouted, "And what makes you think you're going to take voice lessons? I never had voice lessons. You're not going to have them either."

In spite of her opposition, I had a car and a job, and she wasn't going to control my life anymore. I felt it was her cruelty that caused me to be unable to speak properly anyway. I soon discovered that even with professional help, overcoming my speech problems was going to be hard work. The tension in my throat was so great that it took time every session just to get my jaw unlocked and my throat open. I spoke so rapidly that slowing my speech and making it more intelligible took hours of boring practice and then yielded only barely perceptible results. Out of frustration, I ended up in tears after nearly every practice session.

I finally saw the fruit of my labor when I got the lead in the school play and was elected senior class treasurer. Dad was happy for me. Mother was livid.

She continued to remind me that I was still a whore and a slut no matter how many things I accomplished. "You'll never amount to anything, you worthless _____," she would hiss as I left for rehearsal.

The next part of my plan was to earn enough money to afford college. Following my graduation from high school, we moved to a small apartment near Knott's Berry Farm, an amusement park not far from Disneyland, and I found work as an actress and singer in the Bird Cage Theater there. My dad could no longer handle the long hours at the gas station, so he got a regular day job at Knott's as well.

Early one morning on my day off, I decided to clean the tiny room my six-year-old sister and I shared. I couldn't stand her mess any longer. Every drawer on her side of the closet and bedroom were filthy and cluttered with things that should have been trashed long ago. It wasn't her fault. It was part of my mother's neglect of her. Suzy helped me for a while, but then she lost interest and went outside to play. Mother entered as I was putting the finishing touches on the room. She had just awakened, and her eyes were puffy and burned with anger as she demanded, "What do you think you're doing?"

"I've just finished cleaning up our room," I said with pride. I always loved cleaning things and putting them in order. It was one of the many ways I distinguished myself from my mother.

With teeth gritted, her steel-blue eyes burned a hole through my heart as she said, "I told you if I wanted this house clean I would clean it myself. This is not your house, it's mine." Then she went to the closet and pulled out all the books and toys I had so neatly organized on the shelves and threw them on the floor. As she began to empty every drawer of the chest on the floor, something inside of me snapped. This was too much! I began to scream—open-mouthed, hysterical, depth-of-my-being screams.

Then I lunged at her to try and stop her. Quickly her right hand struck me hard across the ear and cheek and part of my eye. The blow stunned me, and before I had time to consider what I was doing, I struck her as hard as I could across the face, the same way she struck me.

She was shocked and so was I. I couldn't believe I had done that. Now my fear of getting stabbed in the middle of the night would be greater. I didn't wait for any further reaction. I grabbed my purse, left the apartment, and drove to a friend's house.

I started to cry in the car and then stopped myself. "She's not worth crying over," I said out loud. "She's just a hateful old witch and not worth my tears. It won't be long before I'm out of there, and then I'll never have to see her again." I came back the next day with my friend, packed some clothes and personal things, and went to stay for a while with her family. When I eventually had to return home, I didn't say anything to my mother and she didn't say anything to me. We focused on Suzy.

After graduation, I enrolled at a state college about 30 minutes from my family's small apartment. Another friend, who was going to the same college, asked me to stay with her and her mother and sister while I attended there. It was one of the greatest times of my life because it was my first experience living in a normal family. They were wonderful, and it brought life to me to see their loving mother-daughter relationships. I saw gentle and consistent signs of love like I'd never seen before.

After that year, I was offered opportunities in the music department at the University of Southern California. The experience of living on campus and going to classes was fantastic, but it was way too expensive, and I decided I was not going to allow myself to stay there beyond that year and be deeply in debt. As it turned out, I was only there a semester because my mother had to have emergency surgery and my dad needed me to move back home to take care of my sister. Even though my mother thought all doctors were out to kill her, apparently the pain she experienced overrode her fear and she submitted to having an operation.

Once I was living back in the apartment, I saw how much my sister had been neglected, and I felt bad for leaving home. But my thinking was if I could get free of poverty myself, then I could help get Suzy out as well. I would get myself through college and then pay for her way through.

I went back to Knott's Berry Farm to work in the Bird Cage Theater again. I did four shows a day—two in the afternoon and two in the evening. My dad worked the early morning shift, so our schedules worked out that someone was always home with Suzy. I also took night classes two nights a week at a local junior college so I wouldn't fall behind.

In the melodrama plays we did at the little theater, I had the part of the heroine, and the actor who played the hero was a handsome, talented comedian named Steve Martin. He was bright and sensitive, and what began as a friendship sharing poetry, philosophy, dreams, and deep thoughts turned into my first head-over-heels-in-love romance. Steve made me feel beautiful, feminine, desirable, and truly loved for the first time in my life. When we were together, time stood still, and there was never anything negative between us. He was refreshingly funny as well as deeply serious and thoughtful. No strife. No pain. No misunderstandings. We were great together. Life was beautiful.

It amazed me that Steve didn't know how gifted, intelligent, and attractive he was. I encouraged him to go to college, expand his mind, set his sights higher than he had, and discover where his talents would lead him. I wanted him to see that he had genius. It was in him already and only needed to be recognized, developed, and defined. He had everything he needed to succeed, and I told him he was destined for greatness. I was certain of it. He had it all.

I didn't realize until Steve wrote his autobiography years later, after he had become hugely successful and famous, that his father had been very disapproving of him. Steve and I never talked about my mother or his father. Both of us were probably still wondering if the opinions and suspicions of those parents would yet prove correct. I could tell his parents liked me, and my parents adored Steve. My mother was actually on her best behavior when he was around. It was impossible for anyone not to like him.

However, we were young and had many dreams and aspirations and knew we had to pursue them. So after our season together, there was no sad breakup, only an uncalculated drift into wherever our lives would take us. It would prove to be the only relationship for which I would have no regrets or bad feelings—only happy memories of good times, kindness, love, and mutual appreciation. His mother and I wrote one another several times a year for decades until she passed away many years later. I think his dad was always waiting for him to get a real job.

I went back to college for my junior year, only this time I went to UCLA. It was a great university, right between Hollywood and Beverly Hills where I wanted to be. And it was far less expensive. I worked to pay for college as I went along, so the only student loan I had was for that one semester at USC.

Later that year at Christmas I received an invitation from my high school boyfriend, Scott Lansdale*, to spend Christmas with him and his family. He attended a prestigious college in the East, and his family had moved to a city in the Midwest. I jumped at the opportunity because any excuse to avoid being around my mother, especially during the holidays, was a good one.

The Lansdales were wealthy, and their home was everything my home was not. It was large, sprawling, beautiful, and clean. Even the large picture windows that looked out over the beautiful manicured lawn were spotless. Scott's parents were normal, and I adored his mother and father. They were intelligent and fun. Scott always teased me, saying I liked his parents more than I liked him. That unfortunately proved to be true. I would have given anything to have traded mothers with him.

Mrs. Lansdale was a gentle, smart, sensitive woman who got up early every morning to fix breakfast. She treated me as if I had great worth, and it was hard not to contrast her to my own mother. We quickly became close friends, but not close enough for me to share the intimate details about my past. It was too embarrassing to tell anyone about being locked in a closet as a child, or having to listen as Mother wandered the house at night, talking to voices that only she heard. If I revealed this to Mrs. Lansdale, she would surely reject me. After all, I reasoned, if a parent rejects you, you must be the rejectable type.

One evening after a big party at the Lansdale house, all the guests had left and Mr. and Mrs. Lansdale went upstairs to bed. Scott and I stayed in the comfortable party room in the basement and had wine by the fire. In my desperation to feel loved, I was careless, and it proved to be a night I would later regret.

A few weeks after returning to L.A., I learned from my father that Mother's condition had worsened. He had consulted a doctor, who diagnosed her mental illness with a string of medical terms, of which "schizophrenic" and "paranoid" were the only ones I understood. So it was officially confirmed that more than just meanness and a hateful disposition were motivating my mother's behavior. There was something definitely wrong with her, something that had a name.

Mental illness was not openly discussed at this time because it didn't produce a sympathetic response. It was a reflection upon family members, as if their sanity was suspect too. Dad and I kept it quiet, and my mother's older sister, my Aunt Margaret*—agreed to fly in to help Dad have Mother committed.

"You need to be there too, Stormie," Margaret instructed me on the phone. "Your mother should know that we are united in our belief that this is what's best for her. The doctors say that if she can be convinced to go on her own to the hospital, half the battle will be won. The response of patients who turn themselves in is far better than those who have to be taken forcibly."

"But she will never go for it. She won't go peaceably, and she will never let you take her."

Everyone but me seemed to think this was a good idea and that she would respond well. However, I knew Mother's dark nature far better than anyone else and was convinced the scene would be ugly.

The date was set for a week later, and I was to meet my aunt at my parents' apartment. It was arranged for my little sister to be away that night. Dad, my aunt, and I would lay out the plan for Mother. She would see the wisdom in it and would go calmly with us as we drove her to the mental hospital.

*They're dreaming,* I thought. *They don't know her at all. My mother is totally convinced that she's right and the rest of the world is wrong, that she's innocent and all others are guilty, that she's normal and everyone else is crazy. There's no way on earth that she'll admit there's something wrong with her.*

In the meantime, as I tried to prepare for finals at the university, I became so sick I couldn't eat or sleep, let alone study. I had grown increasingly ill since the holidays. At first I figured it was stomach flu, but it persisted. I finally went to a doctor and learned, to my horror, that I was pregnant. The news devastated me. How did this happen? I was inexperienced and had trusted Scott to take the necessary precautions.

I stumbled out of the doctor's office and drove to a pretty little church just off campus. I sat in the empty sanctuary and tried to examine my options. None were good.

Marriage was out of the question. While I would have gone for that solution in an instant, I clearly got the message from Scott that he no longer wanted anything to do with me or this problem. He was a brilliant law student, an important man on campus, and the pride of his family. They expected him to become a senator or governor. No way would he throw it all away just to right a little mistake. Besides, he'd proved to be untrustworthy when it was revealed that he was sending the same love letters to another girl as he was sending to me. Unbeknownst to him, the other girl he was sending the same love letter to had become my best friend. She and I compared notes one day and laughed at our discovery. We took revenge by sending identical letters back to him, and laughed about it. But I was saddened by his lack of integrity. He was not who I thought he was.

Suicide was another solution to my terrifying dilemma of being pregnant and unmarried, but what would that do to my sister and father? We were on the brink of having my mother committed to a mental hospital. It would destroy them. But having the baby would be even worse. I was sure my family would rather that I be dead than humiliate them.

Where could I go? What could I do? I slipped off the pew to my knees and prayed. "God, please get me out of this mess," I said, sobbing. "I promise I'll be good."

I don't know how long I knelt and cried and prayed, but when I finally got up, I'd heard no answer and received no peace from God.

After that I became even more nauseated than before. When the day came to confront Mother, Aunt Margaret flew to Los Angeles. I was so sick I could barely drive, but somehow I made the 90-minute trip in the car to my parents' home. My aunt greeted me at the door, and I began to shake. I went into the bathroom to try to pull myself together. I was grateful for her strength and was glad she was there. If only I could tell her the truth and go home with her to the pretty rainbow-colored room I had once stayed in on the second floor of her beautiful house. If only I could crawl between those clean, colorful sheets and pull them over my head until this nightmare went away.

"Oh, God!" I cried. "There is no way out. I'm trapped."

I came out of the bathroom and told my aunt, "I can't stay. I have finals in the morning, and I feel like I am going to throw up. I can't bear to see the scene that's going to be here tonight. Please forgive me, but I have to go. Can you explain it to Dad for me?"

She looked extremely disappointed but promised she would call and let me know what happened.

I made my way back to my UCLA apartment in Westwood Village and threw myself on the bed. I was too sick and distraught to study for finals. I would have to rely on the work I had done all semester to carry me. "Oh, God, give me a good memory." *Why am I praying? Does God hear me? Is there even a God?*

Early the next morning my aunt called. "Are you feeling any better?"

"A little," I lied. "I'm heading for my exam in a few minutes. How did it go last night?"

"Not good. When we approached your mother about going peacefully to the hospital, she became hysterical." Aunt Margaret took a deep breath before continuing. "I've never seen her like that. She screamed at us and said we were just like all the other Communists who were out to kill her. She called us horrible names. You can't believe the things she said."

"Yes, I can. She says those things to me all the time."

"We tried to talk reasonably, but she screamed, '*You're* all crazy, *I'm* not! There is nothing wrong with me.' Then she ran to her room, grabbed her purse and car keys, flew out the door and into the car, and was gone before we could stop her."

"Where is she now?"

"We don't know. She didn't come back last night. The doctor informed your father that he could sign some papers and the police would pick her up and have her committed."

There was silence.

"Well…what did Dad do?"

"He broke down and cried and said he just couldn't do it. He feels that if he has her committed she will never forgive him, and maybe one day she will snap out of it."

I knew he had visions of insane asylums out of the horror movies of the past and felt there would be no hope for her there. As cruel as she had been to him over the years, he still loved her enough to stick it out in hopes that someday she would "snap out of it"—as if that were even possible.

"So it's up to you, Stormie," her deeply exhausted voice continued on the phone. "The only one who can do anything for your mother is you."

"Me?" I choked. "You've got to be kidding. There's nothing I can do with her. We've always hated each other."

"Yes, I know," she said, sighing. "I'm afraid your mother was a terrible mother."

I couldn't believe my ears. Someone else knew she was a terrible mother? I gathered strength from her remark because the recognition of that truth by someone made me feel that I wasn't crazy after all. At the same time, I wondered why my aunt had never reached out to help me.

I felt the responsibility of the world on my shoulders at that point. I was pregnant and sick, and my dad and sister needed me more than ever now that Mother had left. I couldn't disappear for a year to have a baby. My suicide would destroy them. There was only one place left to turn.

# 7

# Choices for Death

"Stormie! How are you?" Julie's* voice chirped over the phone.

"I'm not as good as I'd like to be." I had met Julie the previous summer while working at Knott's Berry Farm. "I really need your help. Do you remember when you confided in me about the abortion you had? Well, I need to get in contact with the doctor who performed it."

I held my breath as I waited for her reply. If she refused to help me, I didn't know where I would go. Abortion was never mentioned in public. In fact, Julie was the only person I had ever heard speak that word to me.

"You know the police are cracking down," she said. "The doctor who did mine was jailed."

"Oh, no! What am I going to do? Please, Julie, I desperately need your help. I've got to find someone who can take care of my situation."

"I have some contacts. Let me see what I can do. Hang on, Stormie. It may take me a few days to get back to you, but I'll call. I promise."

It was two weeks before I heard back from her. During that time, Dad called to tell me that Mother had finally returned home after about ten days. She had disappeared a few times before, but never for so long. As usual, no one asked where she had been or what she had done. We would proceed as always, pretending as though nothing had happened.

The next day Julie got back to me with news. "I've found a doctor just over the Mexican border in Tijuana."

"I don't care where it's done. I don't even care if he's a doctor. I just want out of this misery. How much?"

"Six hundred dollars."

"Six hundred dollars?" I gasped. "I don't even have fifty dollars!" I paused. "Never mind. I'll get it. Tell him yes and let me know when."

I called Scott and asked him point-blank for the money. After some reluctance and questioning as to whether I was really pregnant or just needing some money, he gave in. I was extremely hurt by his remarks, but I took the money from his parents, who were very concerned for me.

With the cash in hand, I drove to a predetermined meeting place in a deserted area off the main highway to Mexico. A man who was the liaison for the doctor met me and another woman traveling with her husband. We were all going to the same place for the same reason. We gave him our money first. Apart from some minor attempts at conversation, no one spoke as we drove for about an hour to the border. I was very afraid, but I decided that no matter what happened, it had to be better than being pregnant and unbearably nauseated every day.

We had no problem at the border; the guards obviously knew the driver. We drove to a small, nondescript house in an old, dirty, residential section of Tijuana. A Mexican woman met us at the door. Once we were in the living room with the door shut and bolted, the doctor came out to greet us.

Because I was so nervous, I volunteered to go first. I was guided to the back of the house via a long, dark hall. I entered what I expected would be a tiny bedroom, but the door opened to a white, hospital-like operating room with all of the medical equipment needed. A nurse in white helped me put on a white hospital gown and lay down on the table as instructed. As the anesthetist put a needle in a vein in my arm, the doctor leaned over me and said kindly, "Oh, by the way, if you die during this operation, I'll have to dump your body out in the desert. You understand that I can't risk danger for myself and the others by giving your body to the police. I just want you to know that going in."

"Does that happen often?" I questioned, my heart filled with fear.

"No, not often," he replied matter-of-factly. "But it does happen. I don't enjoy doing that, but I have no choice."

I prayed silently, *God, please let me live and I'll be good.* I had wanted to die so many times in my life, and now the thought frightened me.

"Ten, nine, eight, seven…" The next thing I remember I was lying in another room with the nurse preparing me to go home. I immediately noticed that for the first time in about four weeks I didn't feel like vomiting. The nightmare was over! It didn't occur to me that I had just destroyed a life. All I could see was that I had escaped death. I had no remorse—only elation that I was still alive and now had a second chance. No one would ever know about this except those involved.

*Thank You, God,* I prayed. *I'll do all the right things. I will appreciate what I have instead of complaining about all I lack. I'll find out more about You, and I won't make the same mistake again.*

The prayer was simplistic but sincere. I meant every promise, but I soon discovered that I was too weak to fulfill any of them. After I returned to school, I fell right back into the same old habits and thought patterns.

That summer I was hired as a singer for a popular new theater-in-the-round that did live musical comedies with different guest stars every two weeks. The hours were long because we rehearsed one show during the day and performed another at night. To save money, I moved back home with my parents, but I was there only to sleep because the drive was more than 90 minutes each way to the theater.

Mother adopted a new policy after she returned home from wherever she had escaped to on the night of the confrontation with her. She stepped up her angry, aggressive hatred toward Dad and backed off on *me*. She now viewed my father and her own sister as her enemies. Because I wasn't present during the night of the horrible scene, I was not considered a traitor. Suzy was never in question. She was neutral ground for everyone.

Many times I found Suzy upset over Mother's bizarre behavior. Because I had basically raised her for the first six years of her life, I had managed to somewhat protect her from Mother's mental problems. But once I started college and was gone a great deal, she had to cope alone. I felt bad about that, but my own education was the next step out of poverty. And hers as well.

Late one night I came home and found Suzy crying. "Are you upset because of Mom?"

"Yes," she said, sobbing.

I hugged her and stroked her hair. "There's something wrong with Mom," I explained. "She's very sick, and she won't go to the hospital. So we have to take care of her as best we can. Try not to take anything she says or does personally because she can't help it."

I couldn't believe how well I had spoken those words. I despised my mother. I didn't have one ounce of pity for her; the only pity I felt was for myself and Suzy. Yet I was convincing enough that my sister was encouraged and seemed to cope better after that.

Suzy's relationship with Mother was never scarred like mine. With me there was irreparable damage because of all the abuse. As a result, I had a hard time coping with life. The emptiness and pain I experienced on a daily basis deepened every year. My anxiety and depression only grew worse, and I faced suicidal thoughts that met me every morning when I awoke. On top of all that, I battled chronic fatigue as I drove myself with constant work in a futile attempt to rise above my condition and not allow it to drown me.

My final show of the summer was *Call Me Madam* with Ethel Merman, a star of legendary status. I loved the show and I loved working with Ethel. The thought of it ending and my going back to UCLA for my senior year was depressing because of the bad memories of the pregnancy, sickness, and the abortion. I needed to escape from that for a season. So when a fellow singer asked if I'd be interested in touring with the Norman Luboff Choir, a group that was very popular then because of their hit songs on the radio, I immediately said yes.

For the next nine months I toured the United States, which presented me with some unanticipated problems. Living with 30 other people in the confines of a bus, without even the luxury of a private room at night, meant that I had to hide my depressions and giant insecurities and put up a good front *all* the time. It was exhausting. It became impossible.

Once a week I would call home to check on my sister. One evening after a show, I called from Georgia and Mother answered the phone. She was livid about my being with Norman Luboff. "Because of your high visibility, they're going to find me and kill me," she snapped. Apparently the fact that she claimed for years "they" were watching her through the TV and had her house bugged didn't matter. "Don't you forget that you are worthless," she continued. "It doesn't matter that you sing with that fancy choir. You're still nothing. A nobody."

Mother was crazy. I knew that. So why was I shaking as I hung up the phone? I recognized that what she was saying was not true, yet I was destroyed every time I heard her words. She still had the power to devastate me, like the little girl she had locked in the closet. When she caught me in a weak moment, she could plunge a knife into my heart and put me into the pit of depression for weeks. Part of me knew she was nuts. The other part believed every word she said. Why did Mother always have this hold over me?

I went downstairs to join some of the singers who were waiting for me in the hotel restaurant. I was so depressed I could barely speak or eat, so I excused myself early, went back to my room, and cried myself to sleep.

By the next morning I had pulled myself together enough to join the group for breakfast. I even manufactured a smile and a few jokes. One of the young men noted, "Ah, I see you're manic today." I found the comment amusing—I even laughed with everyone else at the table—but it was painful. Any reference to my mental instability fed an inherent fear that I might become like my mother.

I came off the tour distraught and mentally, emotionally, and physically exhausted. Trying to maintain a good front had taken its toll. Living in close quarters with people for that length of time only pointed out how odd I was compared to everyone else. I felt like a failure as I went home and basically stayed in bed for several weeks.

I was shaken out of my lethargy one day when I was invited to audition for a new TV musical variety show that CBS was airing in the summer of 1966. I did everything I knew to make myself look and sound good, but when I saw the beauty and talent of the other girls, I was so depressed that I went home and climbed right back into bed.

When the contractor called later to tell me I was chosen as one of the four singers on the show, I was shocked. My joy was immediately mixed with fear. Obviously, I had done a good audition, but how long could I keep up the front? My anxiety attacks were getting worse, and I never knew when they would happen. When they occurred, I had to hide in the nearest bathroom stall, holding my stomach while I convulsed with stifled sobs and feeling as if a sword had been run through my heart. How long could I cover *that* up? Other times when I was afraid, my throat tightened and I would lose my voice. What if that happened on this job?

In spite of all my fears, I accepted the role—I was more afraid not to—and made it somewhat successfully through the summer series. It was a popular show and everyone on it was the best in the business. Bob Mackie was the wardrobe designer and did miracles with a low budget. He would take cheap pieces of leftover fabric and make outfits that looked sensational. After that series ended, I received more opportunities to sing, dance, and act on one TV show after another, along with commercials and record sessions. I performed with stars like Danny Kaye, Jack Benny, Jimmy Durante, George Burns, Dean Martin, Jerry Lewis, Mac Davis, Stevie Wonder, Linda Ronstadt, Sonny and Cher, and many more—all popular at the time. Usually I could summon everything I had for the auditions so they went great. However, when it came time to perform, I struggled with depression and anxiety so badly that they would threaten to ruin everything.

I had retained a good agent to help me with work offers. One evening he called. "Why did you turn down the part in that movie today, Stormie?" Jerry* demanded. "After all your auditioning and my hard work you just walked out on the offer. I can't understand what is the matter with you."

"I'm sorry, Jerry." I searched desperately for an answer that would explain it. "At the last minute I just couldn't go through with it."

"Go through with what? You had the part. All you had to do was show up for work."

"I know. I'm sorry, Jerry. I'm really sorry."

After a long silence in which I could almost hear his mind trying to make sense of the things I did to jeopardize my own career, he said goodbye and hung up.

It was impossible for anyone to understand my inconsistencies. I could hardly understand them myself. For years I had dreamed of doing the things I was now doing. But all of the modeling, commercials, television shows, and acting could not convince me I was attractive or talented. No matter what glamorous and wonderful things happened to me, I still saw myself as ugly and unacceptable—a failure who would never amount to anything, as my mother always reminded me. Just a few hours after the ecstasy of attaining a new goal, I felt worse than ever because I thought, *If this doesn't make me feel better, what will? Why can't I change myself? Why am I so damaged? Why can't I escape my past?*

I kept looking for the perfect relationship, always thinking that it would make a difference. Appearances meant a lot to me, so I picked men who seemed sophisticated, educated, and cultured. I wanted to be part of any lifestyle that was opposite to the way I grew up. Tommy* fit the bill perfectly. He was handsome, kind, a gentleman, and he worked a lot as a singer in Hollywood.

We were actually a total mismatch, but I couldn't allow myself to recognize that. I figured I would always be a mismatch with anyone great. I wanted to be loved unconditionally and be touched emotionally, but Tommy only wanted a good time, and any suggestion of commitment or marriage drove him away. I knew he wasn't good for me, yet his kindness, attractive appearance, and flamboyant lifestyle made me want to believe that eventually he could fulfill my need for love and security.

All my grasping for love caused me to end up in the same situation that two years earlier I had promised God would never happen again. I got pregnant. Oddly enough, precautions were used both times, and both had failed. I couldn't believe it.

As before, I had nowhere to go and no one who wanted me in that condition.

But this time my main concern was for my career. Getting pregnant was definitely a bad career move, and without my career I would cease to exist. To make things even more complicated, I was scheduled to tour Europe, Africa, and South America for the next three months with a well-known singing group who had hit records at the time. I was leaving within the week, so I had to act quickly.

This pregnancy made me even sicker than before. The abortionist in Mexico was nowhere to be found, so on the recommendation of a knowledgeable source I flew to Las Vegas to try and make a connection with a certain doctor there. Tommy gladly agreed to pay for it, even though I could afford it myself by this time.

I went to this doctor's office and begged him to do the operation. He was suspicious of me because I didn't work or live in Las Vegas, and he wanted to run a test to determine for sure that I was pregnant.

"How long will it take to get the results back?"

"Two to three days."

"I can't wait that long. I'm leaving on a three-month singing tour out of the country in two days. I need the operation right away."

"This is a setup, isn't it?"

"What do you mean?" I asked. Then I realized he thought I might be part of an undercover sting by the police.

He remained thoughtful and silent for a moment and then said, "No, I can't do it."

"Please," I begged him. "If you won't do it, send me to someone who will. I'm desperate. I have the cash."

He remained firm in his decision and left the room.

Later that afternoon, I got a phone call at the place where I was staying. The voice on the other end of the line said, "Do you need a doctor?"

"Yes. Please, can you help me?"

"I have a doctor who will do it. Twelve hundred, cash."

"I've got it. How soon can it be done?"

"I'll pick you up at three o'clock."

Suddenly I felt scared. "This is a real doctor, right? And he'll put me to sleep and I won't feel any pain?"

"Of course," the voice mumbled and hung up.

At three o'clock a short, stocky, balding man came to my door. He was nervous and constantly mopped his sweaty forehead with a dirty white handkerchief. I got in his car and we drove a short distance to an obscure, low-class motel near the center of town. We entered through the back door and took the elevator to the second floor. He had a room key, and we quickly entered one of the rooms. Until now I had thought this operation would be a breeze like last time, but as we entered the sleazy motel room I knew I was wrong.

"Where's the doctor?" I asked, panicking. "Where's the anesthesiologist? Where's the equipment?"

"Shh! You gotta be quiet. People will hear you," he snapped. "The doctor will be in as soon as you're ready. Let me see the cash."

I gave him the money.

"Take off your clothes from the waist down and lay faceup on that low chest of drawers."

"You've got to be kidding! Where is the doctor? I want to see him first."

"Look, do you want the operation or not!" he asked gruffly.

Seeing no alternative, I did as he said. The man then put a blindfold tightly around my eyes and tied a gag over my mouth. "You must not see the doctor or make any noise," he explained. "These operations are extremely dangerous now. The police are cracking down. We can't give you an anesthetic because we must move fast if there's any problem. Believe me, this is the best way."

I was numb with fright as he tied me to the top of the chest of drawers. No anesthetic? My heart pounded wildly. I didn't know this man. He could kill me and take my money right there. Then I heard the door open quietly and someone else entered the room. The two of them whispered briefly, and I could tell the other person was a man. Soon I heard the clanking of surgical tools.

Then the real nightmare began. The first man placed himself across the top half of my body while the "doctor" began the work of the abortion. As he scraped and cut, I began to cry. I gagged and retched and experienced the most excruciating pain of my life. It seemed endless. I groaned so loudly that the man placed the full force of his chest over my face to stifle the sounds. I was afraid I might smother. Finally, there was one excruciating cut on the inside that felt that it must have severed the baby from the uterine wall. It was beyond any pain I could possibly have imagined. A few seconds later it was over, and the doctor left the room.

The man untied me, took off the blindfold and gag, and then the phone rang. He answered it, but I was in such pain and shock that I didn't notice what he said. I slid off the chest and stumbled toward the bed for my clothes. Nausea, sobs, and pain racked my whole body.

The man hung up the phone, turned to me, and said angrily, "Clean up this mess. The police are downstairs, and the place is swarming with FBI agents."

Just as he said that, I threw up all over the bed and my clothes. Vomit and blood covered my legs. The man, full of disgust, cleaned up the mess around the chest of drawers. What had been cut out of my body lay in bloody paper towels on the floor, and he wanted that evidence against him destroyed. "Finish cleaning up and flush everything down the toilet," he sternly instructed as he fled from the room.

I did not want to be found in this condition either, so as sick as I was, I followed his instructions. With towels from the bathroom, I wiped the blood and vomit from my legs, the bed, the chest of drawers, and the floor. I cleaned off my clothes as best I could and hurriedly put them back on. Tears mixed with sweat and mascara ran down my face. I was still convulsing with sobs.

The man came back relieved. "There was a kidnapping downstairs. It has nothing to do with us. I'll finish cleaning this place; you go fix your face and hair." A few minutes later he drove me back to where I was staying.

In contrast to the last abortion, when I felt relieved to be alive, this time I felt depression, failure, and disgust. It had been so ugly.

A couple of days later, I flew from Las Vegas to the East Coast to begin a world tour with that popular singing group. My bleeding continued for weeks, and eventually I had to enter a hospital for an operation to stop it. But the pain of the memory never stopped. Every time I saw a baby I felt it all over again. I mourned and felt an emptiness unlike any I had ever known. I wasn't the same after that. Mentally, I began to spiral downward.

Would there ever be an end to the hopelessness I felt, or was I doomed to this kind of painful existence for as long as I lived? Where could I find answers? Who could help me?

I returned home from the tour to the apartment in Hollywood that I had rented with my best friend from high school. Diana* had acted with me in the school plays, and that was where we first met. She and I had the two leads in one of the productions, and we hit it off right away. She was extremely bright and talented, but she suffered with depression and anxiety too. She felt I was trustworthy enough to share that her mother was a raging alcoholic, and that's why she could never bring anyone over to her house. I shared with her about my situation with my mentally ill mother, and that's why I could never have anyone over either. Experiencing abuse at the hands of our mothers and having pacifistic fathers bonded us. We totally understood each other. She told me she thought she must have been adopted. Her father confirmed that to me and described how as a child she went searching through the house for the adoption papers.

She went to college in San Francisco while I stayed in Southern California, so we lost track of each other for several years. When I was looking in Hollywood for an apartment, I walked from building to building in the area where I wanted to live, seeing what was available. In one place I saw a great apartment, but I needed a roommate to live there in order to share the expenses. The manager of the next building I went to look at wasn't in, but as I was leaving I happened to look at the tenant registry, and there was Diana's name. I knew it had to be her because her last name was very unusual.

I knocked on her door and she answered. We were both shocked and delighted to see each other. Her apartment was a crowded, dark, one-room place, and I thought about the larger, newer, sunny apartment I had seen with a sliding glass door leading to an outdoor balcony with somewhat of a view. After we talked a little and reconnected as if we had never been separated, I told her about the great apartment I had just seen and asked her if she would share it with me. She said she gladly would.

When I walked in the door of our apartment after this three-month tour in South America, South Africa, England, and France, my depression and exhaustion were so strong I just wanted to go to sleep and wake up weeks later. Diana met me at the door, and she looked even more haggard than I did. She'd gained a lot of weight, and that was always a sign that depression had overtaken her.

I walked to the refrigerator for something to eat or drink, but it was empty except for a diet cola and some unhealthy diet drink. I could see that everything was filthy. Dust an inch thick was everywhere, and the kitchen was a disaster. It looked as though she had done nothing to clean any part of the apartment the entire time I was gone. That only added to the despair I felt. It didn't seem hopeful to be living with someone who was even more hopeless than I was.

I didn't say anything about all of that. I was way too tired to go out and find food, so I went to bed hungry, deciding I would get groceries and clean the apartment when I woke up. My depression was black. The only thing that got me out of bed the next day was hunger and an allergy to dust.

The rest of the tour was canceled when one of the three guys contracted a serious illness. I was now without work, and being on the road for so long causes people to forget about you back in town. I had to gear myself up to start auditions again. Diana soon decided to escape into a marriage that was doomed to fail—which it did. But by that time I had moved to a tiny apartment in the Hollywood Hills alone, and work started coming in.

# 8

# Truth Without Freedom

D r. Foreman, the kind psychologist, listened to my story unfold over a number of months, and he helped me to gain some perspective about what had happened to me. Now I could see where my fears came from and how they controlled me. Talking with him was a relief, for no matter what I told him, he never made me feel that I was crazy or deserving of judgment.

Neither of us, however, could understand the origin of my mother's hatred and why she treated me the way she did. Yes, she was mentally ill, but mental illness doesn't usually result in cruelty and violence. I had an unshakable desire to find out more about her.

Dr. Foreman thought it was an excellent idea for me to travel to where my mother's family was so I could talk to them and find out how she came to be this way. I flew to Nebraska and talked with my mother's father, her two sisters, aunts, and cousins. It was difficult putting all of the pieces together because everyone remembered the past a little differently. Dr. Foreman had warned me that seven members of a family will give seven different accounts of the same event. It certainly proved true in this case, but one thing that was consistent was that everyone cried as they spoke of my mother and the past. The tragedy of her life could not be ignored.

I didn't tell anyone my purpose for being there. How could I add to their hurt by saying that Mother had abused me and now I was trying to rise above the scars? How could I say that my life was falling apart and I was seeing a psychologist to help me pull it together? By this time I knew I wasn't crazy, but I did have serious doubts that I could ever be normal. My only hope was that I would learn to cope.

After a week of questions, I was able to somewhat piece together my mother's life. Although it was apparent she was not abused as a child, her life was definitely scarred by trauma.

She was born the middle child of three girls. She was beautiful and well-liked but also stubborn, lazy, and obstinate. Her bright and lively personality made a good impression at social gatherings, but on a one-to-one basis with certain members of the family she was cruel and cold. During the Depression people were concerned with survival, so the emotional state of a family member wasn't a priority. As a result, her undesirable character traits and strong will usually went unchallenged.

When she was 11, she had an unpleasant encounter with her mother, who was 9 months pregnant at the time. Apparently, her mother verbally rebuked her for something she had done. But my mother stomped her feet and talked back saying, "You're wrong! I didn't do it!" She was sent to her room, where she silently wished her mother was dead. A few hours later her mother went into labor, and at the hospital she died in childbirth along with the baby.

As children frequently do, my mother felt responsible for what happened and believed her mother's death was both a punishment for her rebellious attitude and a rejection of her. Uncensored guilt and unbearable grief led to deep emotional scarring from which she never recovered.

The shock of his wife's death overwhelmed my mother's father, and the burden of caring for his three daughters was more than he could handle. The girls were separated and passed around among different relatives and friends. Because of that, my mother felt abandoned, isolated, and alone. Again, this was during the Depression, and having an extra child to feed and clothe was not always considered a blessing. My mother knew that the various foster parents she stayed with favored their natural children over her, as shown in their affection and material provision. Whether true or not, this is what she believed, and these perceived injustices instilled in her great anger and bitterness.

She became attached to one certain family in which the other young girls were attractive and possessed qualities that she greatly desired. She tried to emulate them and did her best to make the whole family like her, but just as she was allowing herself to have strong feelings for each member, the father of that family killed himself. No one knew the exact reason for the suicide, but many people suspected it was his financial problems. My mother once again assumed that it was because of her. "I'm responsible for all the deaths in my family," she often told me gravely. I now understood why she thought that way.

Gradually, it became too hard for my mother to cope with the real world. She believed she was responsible for the deaths of two of the most important people in her life, and because she was at an age where she was unable to understand or verbalize her feelings, rejection took root. With everyone around her forced to deal with serious problems of their own, there was no one to help *her*. Unable to cope with the mountain of guilt she faced daily, she withdrew from reality into a world of her own making where she was blameless and perfect.

During her late teenage years, my mother contracted a severe case of scarlet fever and came close to death. When she recovered, certain close family members told me that she was never the same after that. Her emotional instability became more apparent, and her already changeable personality exhibited hot and cold mood swings that defied logic. She tried desperately to get out of the small town where she lived to attend college or study music, but there was no money for that. Besides, her father strongly opposed it. He firmly believed it was pointless to waste money educating a woman, for she would just get married and have babies anyway. This added to her growing frustration, bitterness, and insecurity.

As a child, my mother had been put in a closet a few times by her father as punishment for minor infractions. Even though those incidents were infrequent and of short duration, she was severely indignant and vocal about her dislike of them. She was jealous of both her sisters, and she had mentioned to me many times how she felt they had consistently received better treatment. But I heard the exact opposite from them; they claimed *she* was the favored one. I believed them. Because of that belief, she was especially cruel to her younger sister, and when she had to babysit her she put her in a closet a number of times for punishment. It helped me greatly to know that.

After hearing these stories, I began to feel sorry for my mother. She was someone to be pitied instead of hated. She had been trapped by her environment and the circumstances surrounding her life. A stronger person may have worked through the problems, but she survived the only way she knew how, and her mistreatment of me was a kind of payback for all of the times she was rejected.

This didn't excuse her actions, but it made them more understandable. I believe she locked me in a closet so she could better cope with life, and she simply forgot how long I was left there. She was angry at her mother for dying, angry at her dad for not helping her when she needed him most, angry at the suicide of the father figure she had in the foster family, angry at her sisters, who she thought were favored over her, and angry at God for the circumstances of her life. She was filled with repressed rage, which she vented on the most likely recipients—her younger sister, me, and later my dad.

Many people realized that Mother was mentally unstable, but few knew how bad she was because of her ability to appear so normal at times. Even the ones who were aware of her bizarre behavior did not recognize the seriousness of her illness. Out of curiosity, I asked certain people when they first realized that my mother was different. I received a variety of answers.

"When she was in her late teens," said her younger sister, "right after she had scarlet fever."

"She was always emotionally fragile," said her older sister.

"After she had been married a short while," said many.

"She was physically frail from the beginning," said her father, "and her personality was always difficult. It's hard to believe that her mind has deteriorated this badly…" His sad voice trailed away.

The night before I was to leave, I lay in bed and thought about all I had heard. I recalled a rare conversation I'd had alone with my dad early one morning before Mother was awake. "When did you first realize there was something wrong with Mother?" I boldly questioned him.

"I noticed it on our honeymoon. She thought someone was following us and refused to stop at the hotel where we had reservations. We traveled to four different hotels before I finally told her that we were not going to another hotel." He knew no one was following them and couldn't understand why she was behaving that way.

I was completely shocked that he had known about this from the day they were married. I silently questioned his judgment while marveling that he had put up with her for so long. He must have really loved her to overlook all of that.

As I turned out the light and pulled the covers up to my chin, I felt troubled. There were no clear-cut answers about Mother. Was she born with a chemical imbalance, or did the trauma of her childhood cripple her? Was her brain damaged by the high fever during her bout with scarlet fever? Did she have signs of mental illness way back in her teens that no one recognized? Was it all of these things? I couldn't answer those questions, nor could anyone else.

I thought that knowing the truth would make a difference, but it didn't change the way I felt inside. All of that information only stirred up my own pain even more.

I still felt like a prisoner of my past. I thought, *I understand everything, yet I understand nothing.*

I cried into my pillow as despair overtook what little hope had been raised over the last few months. "What am I supposed to do now?" I sobbed to no one.

# 9

# Finding the One True Light

I flew home more miserable than before I left. Rick had not lifted a finger to keep the house clean while I was gone, so it was a mess when I arrived. I looked at my house and my life, and I couldn't cope with either of them anymore.

I stared into the bathroom mirror as I undressed for bed. I looked old. My skin was sallow, wrinkled, and broken out. The pores were large. My hair was dry and thinning. Prematurely gray hairs had steadily increased in my twenties with every new trauma. My mind was also gray. There were no bright colors in my life. My eyes were dull and lifeless, with dark circles under them that I could no longer hide with makeup. I was 28 years old, but I looked 40.

My health was not responding to good nutrition and exercise as it had in the past. I had a sinus infection and constant low-grade nausea that had both gone on for months. I felt unloved, undesirable, unattractive, and more locked up than ever. My emptiness knew no bounds. I saw only the hopelessness of my life. All my methods for survival had failed. A new season of *The Glen Campbell Goodtime Hour* was due to start in a few weeks, but this time I didn't think I could pull it together again.

*God,* I said silently, *I don't want to live anymore. Things will never get better and life makes no sense. Please let me die.*

Suicide was the answer. Only this time I wasn't going to slip up. It would be clean. I would arrange for all my money to go to Dad and Suzy, and the death would look like an accidental overdose of drugs and booze. I would be out of my misery without inflicting pain on anyone else. I made plans to secure enough pills to do the job. I was dying every day anyway, so why not end this torture?

The next night my Christian friend, Terry, called me to do another record session as a background singer. During a break she abruptly said, "I can see you're not doing well, Stormie. Why don't you come with me and meet my pastor? He's a wonderful man and I know he can help you."

I hesitated.

"What have you got to lose?" she insisted. "I'll pick you up and take you. Okay?"

I looked at the devastation of my life and clearly saw that she was right—I certainly had nothing to lose. "Okay," I said simply.

Two days later Terry picked me up and drove me to a popular restaurant, where we met Pastor Jack. He was a warm, effervescent man with a direct gaze, and he exuded a confidence that might have been intimidating had it not been tempered by an obviously loving and compassionate heart. He spoke with a remarkable balance of eloquence and clear, down-to-earth communication. Although he was possibly ten years older than I was, everything about him was youthful. I kept looking for phoniness, shady motives, discrepancies, or manipulation, but I never found any of that. He was unlike anyone I'd ever met in my life.

Pastor Jack listened intently as I shared briefly about my depression and fear. I was still trying to keep up a good front, even at this late hour in my life. I didn't want either of them to know I was nauseated and fighting an infection that wasn't responding to any method of treatment. I saw any admission of weakness as a sign of failure. I definitely didn't want them to know the details of my mother and my childhood and the horrible things I had done.

Pastor Jack worked his way into a conversation about God with such ease that it was as though he was talking about his best friend. He made God sound like a touchable person who cared.

"How much do you know about Jesus, Stormie?"

"Just a few details," I said, recalling my past experience with church. "I know about His birth in a stable and that He was put to an undeserved and cruel death on a cross. He was supposed to have been a good man. Other than that, I really know nothing."

"Have you ever heard of the term 'born again'?"

I looked at him with a vague expression. "I've heard of it, but I don't know what it means."

"Jesus said that He was the Son of God, and that unless we are born again, we cannot see the kingdom of God," the pastor explained. "Jesus said that His Father's will is that everyone who looks to the Son and believes in Him shall have eternal life. Looking to the Son means accepting Him as Savior and thereby being born again into God's kingdom. It's a spiritual birth, not a physical birth. It's the opportunity to not only secure your eternal future, but your future in this life as well. You can begin life anew, and your past will be forgiven and buried."

I was fascinated by that, and especially when he spoke about how God's Holy Spirit would come into my life and transform me from the inside out. I longed for such a thing, but I'd never dreamed it was possible.

"Being born again happens in the spirit realm," he went on, "but it affects your situation and your physical life in practical ways as well."

Pastor Jack never asked me if I wanted to identify with Jesus; rather, he talked *about* Him as one would tell stories about a beloved family member. This was different from the many times when people had walked up to me on the street, pushing a piece of paper in my face and talking harshly and lovelessly about repentance, sin, and salvation. They seemed to think of themselves as superior over those who weren't like them, and because of that I had wanted no part of their lifestyle. But this was different.

Two hours flew by, and near the end of our time together, Pastor Jack asked me, "Do you like to read?"

"I love to read!" I responded eagerly.

"If I give you some books, would you read them this week?"

"Sure."

Terry and I followed him to his office at the church, where he carefully selected three books from his well-stocked shelves. Handing them to me, he said, "Let's meet back at the restaurant in exactly one week. I want to hear what you think of these."

"Great!" I said with enthusiasm. My new reading assignment gave me something tangible to look forward to.

Talking with Pastor Jack and Terry had been a welcome reprieve from the torturous oppression in my life, but it ended when I returned home. As Terry drove off, the nausea returned, and I couldn't wait to climb into bed.

I began reading the books the next day, soaking in their contents like a sponge. It was as if I was transported out of my dreary life into another world.

The first book was *The Screwtape Letters* by C.S. Lewis. It's a characterization about a devil who wrote letters of instruction to his nephew. The letters spoke of how to destroy people by setting traps and waiting for victims to fall into them. Of course, I was educated and sophisticated enough to not believe in a devil. After all, didn't my occult practices and religions teach me that there was no evil force except what existed in my own mind? So the idea of a devil was amusing yet fascinating. As certain real-life situations were presented in the story, C.S. Lewis seemed to have a logical, almost believable explanation for them. I instantly related to many of them.

The second book was about the work of the Holy Spirit. Again, even though I had heard about the "Father, Son, and Holy Spirit," I'd never thought of the Holy Spirit as the Spirit of God who dwells in us when we open up to receive Jesus, and that He has the power to change lives and guide and comfort us. This, too, was fascinating and seemed logical.

The third book was the Gospel of John, which is the fourth book of the New Testament in the Bible, but it was presented to me in the form of a separate short book. I read it in one sitting, and the words on each page came alive with meaning. I felt the vitality of those words somehow entering my heart and bringing life to me.

Jesus said, "I have come as a light into the world, that whoever believes in Me should not abide in darkness."[1] I immediately recognized something. I had been living in darkness all of my life. I thought, *I know it. I feel it. If I put my faith in Jesus, does that mean He becomes light in my life?*

By the end of the week I was feeling a little better physically, so when Terry and I again met Pastor Jack at the same restaurant, I was eager to talk. We ordered lunch and then he looked at me in his direct manner and said, "Well, what did you think of the books?"

"I believe they are the truth."

He smiled and let me continue.

"I don't know why, though. I don't believe in the devil."

He smiled again, unflinching at anything I said, and calmly explained that the way I believed was exactly one of the traps C.S. Lewis had written about.

"The devil wants you to believe that he doesn't exist, that Jesus isn't the Son of God, and that there is no Holy Spirit working with power in your life today, for then he's rendered you totally powerless," he explained.

I began to see the wisdom in what he was saying. And I recognized that I was caught in that trap. I remember reading in the book of John where it said, "In Him was life, and the life was the light of men."[2] I didn't fully understand that. But the next verse said, "The light shines in the darkness, and the darkness did not comprehend it."[3] His light had been there all along, but I couldn't see it. My spiritual eyes had been so blinded that I had chosen darkness over His light, and I didn't even know it.

It was all becoming clearer to me.

Pastor Jack talked more about life and God in a way that made me wish I could see life as he did.

After we finished lunch, he invited us back to his office to pray. Seated across his desk from Terry and me, Pastor Jack looked directly at me and said, "Stormie, you said you believe the books I gave you were the truth. Does this mean you want to receive Jesus today and be born again?"

"Yes, I do," I said softly, and surprisingly without any hesitation.

He led me in a prayer, and I repeated after him: "Jesus, I acknowledge You this day. I believe You are the Son of God as You say You are. Although it's hard to comprehend love so great, I believe You laid down Your life for me so that I might have eternal life with You and an abundant life now. I confess my failures and that I am a sinner. I ask for Your forgiveness. Come into my heart and fill me with Your Holy Spirit. Let all the death in my life be crowded out by the power of Your presence, and turn my life into a new beginning."

It was simple and easy. I was born again, and according to the Bible, I was the Lord's and His Spirit lived in me. "If anyone does not have the Spirit of Christ, he is not His." [4] And that is how I knew the Lord would never leave me nor forsake me, and how He would change me from the inside out. I left Pastor Jack's office feeling light and hopeful and appreciative of that beautiful October day, even though I still didn't fully understand what it all meant.

Terry invited me to come to church with her and her husband on Sunday, and I accepted. They saw I was not strong enough emotionally or physically to make it there on my own, so they came to my house and picked me up. It had been years since I'd been inside a church, and when I entered this one I noticed immediately that it was unlike any I'd ever seen before. The structure and decor were plain compared to the fancy churches I'd been in, although it was neat, pretty, and clean.

"So glad that you're here!" bubbled one of the hostesses as I entered the front door. Though I was wearing jeans and a T-shirt and the hostess was in her Sunday best, she wrapped her arms around me and gave me a big hug. I appraised her cautiously and decided that her smile was genuine and her motive pure. I soon discovered that her friendliness and caring quality were typical of nearly everyone there. It was hard to ignore the exuberance, the laughter, and the absolute joy of life that came from the 300 or so people in the crowded sanctuary. I felt as if I were attending a party compared with the somber churches I had been in years earlier.

As I settled onto one of the comfortable seats near the front, I sensed a spirit of peace descend over my mind. I felt strength coming into me just from being there. Spiritual things were not foreign to me, because I knew there was a spirit realm from all my occult practices, but this was totally different.

Instead of the fear I had previously associated with anything spiritual, I now sensed a supernatural presence of love so powerful that it permeated the air and washed over me.

I felt that I was finally home.

*There's life here,* I thought to myself. *And this life is real.*

# 10

# Not Guilty by Association

Pastor Jack stepped onto the platform of the small sanctuary and began to lead the congregation in songs of worship to God. The singing of hymns and choruses of praise were so powerful that they nearly elevated me out of my shoes. As the voices rose, so did my spirits, and I couldn't help but compare them with the painfully timid congregations I had heard in the past that barely mumbled the words into their hymnals while an overzealous soprano dominated our attention. Again, the words "new life" came to my mind as I tried to label the comparison.

"All hail the pow'r of Jesus' Name! Let angels prostrate fall," the full voices soared in almost a shout. "Bring forth the royal diadem, and crown Him Lord of all!"

And then there was another song about people with broken hearts not having to cry anymore because Jesus had healed them. These words came during a more tender moment. I was affected so profoundly that often I couldn't sing at all but only listen and weep as the worshipping voices penetrated every fiber of my being. I gained healing for my heart and mind from each new song, and I felt a release of tension from down deep inside as stress oozed out of my body.

"The Bible says to lift up holy hands to the Lord," directed Pastor Jack, so I, along with everyone else, responded with upraised hands of worship. When I did that, I felt as if I had just let go of the heavy burdens I had been carrying. I offered them up to God and felt Him take them from me. My tears flowed like a river.

When the worship time ended, Pastor Jack began to speak, and it seemed as if he were speaking directly to me. The Bible, or "Scriptures" as he called them, came alive as he taught on a story that happened thousands of years ago but had a direct bearing on my life right then. He told of the Israelites being set free from Egyptian captivity and then wandering around in the desert for 40 years because they wouldn't listen to God and do things His way.

*That's me*, I thought. *I've been doing things my own way and wandering around in a wilderness. Oh, God, I want to do things Your way now.*

As we were in the car heading home, Terry said, "Well, what did you think?"

I thought for just a moment, and then I replied, "I think I'd better not go to church anymore without waterproof mascara and a box of Kleenex."

She just laughed. She was well aware of how much I was moved by the worship, the teaching, and the powerful presence of the Spirit of God in the service.

I was eager to return the following Sunday and every Sunday after that. For a long time I was still too weak to make it on my own, so Terry got me out of bed with a phone call and picked me up at my house. Every time I entered the church, peace overtook me. Healing and strength came in waves, and I got glimpses of hope for my life.

Never had I heard as great a teacher as Pastor Jack, and I hung on his every word. He always brought the teaching around to where I was living, as if he had prepared his sermon to speak directly to my need. Later I realized that it was the Holy Spirit working in my life and everyone else felt the same way. At the end of each sermon, as the point was driven home, I had to fight back convulsive sobs. But this time of crying always cleansed and healed me, and I sensed a refreshing and renewal in my being when it was over.

Whenever Pastor Jack invited the congregation to receive Jesus, I silently made that commitment again. Just hearing that because of Jesus I could be forgiven of everything I had ever done wrong, and that now I could make a fresh start, brought life to my entire being.

Every time I entered the church I cried. It was the cry of a lost child who had been wandering for a long time, and though she had tried to keep herself strong throughout her wandering, the minute she saw that her daddy had found her, she sobbed. Every Sunday I realized all over again that my heavenly Father had found me. Or I finally found Him. God loved and cared about me when I couldn't love and care about myself.

Unfortunately, the jolt back to "real life" started as soon as Terry drove me home from church. The moment I entered my house, I began to descend slowly back into depression until by the following Sunday morning I could barely get out of bed. Gradually, however, the peace carried over a little longer, until eventually it lasted all of Sunday. Even Rick couldn't destroy it. However, the more joyful I became, the more he retreated in the opposite direction. His negative attitude fully blossomed, and he became more difficult and critical, finding nothing good to say about me or to me.

One morning I came home from church bubbling over with the joy I felt inside. Rick was watching television and made no attempt at communication.

"Rick, this church is so great! I feel wonderful when I come out of there! I wish you'd come with me just one time."

"I've told you before, I don't want to talk about it," he snapped. "If you want to waste time with your creepy Christian friends, that's your business, but leave me out of it."

"Rick, please let me tell you about Jesus," I persisted in hopes of penetrating the wall of his emotions with the truth I'd found. "Jesus has changed my life—"

He suddenly stood and growled with anger in his eyes, "Don't you *ever* mention that name in this house again!" He stomped out of the room, leaving me feeling as though I'd been slapped in the face, and the door shut on what little communication possibilities were left to us. His anger was so intense that I knew I could never mention Jesus to him again. All that remained between us now was resentment. We seldom spoke to one another after that.

As my internal being became more solid and healed, the externals of my life began to change. Little by little some of my bad habits disappeared without my even trying. I refused cigarettes, alcohol, and drugs from old working buddies who thought I was really getting weird.

In a short time, I lost all the close friends I'd had. Not one remained except Terry and my friend Diana, who was divorced and remarried by this time. She didn't reject me when I told her how I had found new life in Jesus. She knew me well enough to see the difference in me, even though she couldn't understand it.

About that time *The Glen Campbell Goodtime Hour* was canceled. Plus, the two main recording and TV contractors I had worked for in Hollywood both developed cancer and died. A singing duo I had performed in for several years in some of the nightclubs around town suddenly dissolved. My commercial agent became irate when I turned down one spot after another.

"Stormie, this is the sixth commercial interview you've refused to go on because it involves liquor, cigarettes, or costumes you think are too revealing." She was obviously disgusted with me. "If you can't accept these opportunities, then there is absolutely nothing we can do for you. We'll send you a release from your contract in the mail." Then she hung up on me.

I placed the receiver in the phone's cradle, stunned by what had just transpired. Part of me felt great relief, but the other part was afraid because my last avenue of revenue was shut off. Suddenly, there was no money coming in, and I knew I could no longer support Rick in that big house. The pressure to come up with all of the money we needed each month was more than I could bear. That, coupled with the fact that he was becoming even more critical and cruel, pushed me to the edge. Life seemed hopeless when I was around him, for he was a constant reminder of all my failures and what a rejected person I had been.

That afternoon I found an apartment and hired an inexpensive moving company to do a small move on short notice. That night I informed Rick I was moving out the next morning. We hadn't even been married the two years I'd planned, but I couldn't take any more of it. I told him he could have the house and everything in it that was his. I would take only what I had brought into our home when we were married or I had purchased since then.

He agreed, and he appeared to take the news very calmly. But I knew he was concerned about having to find a job and pay his own bills. I was so wrapped up in my own feelings that I couldn't see that he battled with self-doubt too. I still couldn't discern anyone else's problems but my own.

I moved the next morning. Because I had only a few possessions, within one day I'd hung every picture and put away every book and dish. Because the entire TV and recording industry in town was very slow at that time, all of my close friends were out of town on tour. I had no one to talk to, so my relief over not having to support Rick and that house was mixed with loneliness. I felt that my life had been turned upside down, and everything that didn't belong in it was shaken out. The only problem was that there was nothing much left — just the church and the Lord.

They were my refuge and only place of security and peace.

During one Sunday morning service while the congregation was praying in small groups, Pastor Jack walked to the back of the church where I was and whispered that he wanted to see me in his office as soon as possible. I was excited to go because I loved him, and any chance to talk to him was welcome. Besides, I had written my first two Christian songs and could hardly wait to show him.

Once we were in the office, his mood became very serious. Pastor Jack was not interested in my songs, but only in the fact that I had filed for divorce. "God's ways don't allow for divorce, Stormie." Then he showed me Scriptures to back that statement up and spent an hour explaining them.

I didn't attempt to blame Rick, nor did I try to explain anything. I took full responsibility for the marriage and its failure. Whatever penalty there was for deceiving Rick into marrying me, I was willing to pay it, even though that thought was terrifying. My choices, as I saw them, were to go back and live with Rick, or else give up my salvation and the church and get a divorce. I knew there was only one choice: I would never go back and live in hell with Rick.

As if he'd read my mind, Pastor Jack's face softened as he leaned forward across his desk and said, "I know you would rather die than go back to a situation where you've been so miserable."

"I can never go back," I said, suppressing my tears. It was still important for me to keep up a good front, so I struggled to keep from crying. I was grateful that he understood my feelings, and if I had to leave the church, at least he knew the reason.

Then he did something totally unexpected. He came over beside my chair, got down on his knees, put his arms around me, gave me a firm hug, and said, "I want you to know that whatever you decide, I still love you, God still loves you, and this church is still your home."

Now I could no longer control the tears that poured down my cheeks. Never had I faced such unconditional love. I tried with all my might to choke back the immense swell of uncontrollable sobs that lay just below the surface. *If I let them loose, Pastor Jack might see what an emotional mess I am and change his mind about letting me stay in this church,* I reasoned. And I could see his secretary in the outer office through the wide-open door. I wondered what she must think of me.

I left with a promise to return for more counseling, and I considered it a great victory that I had not completely fallen apart. I was grateful to God that I didn't have to leave the church and that I could be loved even when I failed. It was my first experience with the unconditional love of God, the depth of which I had never before imagined. I expected judgment. That was what I lived with before I met Jesus. Instead, I found mercy. I had been declared not guilty by association—with Jesus. And I was soon to discover that this acquittal went far deeper than I even dreamed possible.

# 11

# Meeting the Deliverer

I woke up with a start on Sunday morning a few months after I had moved into my new apartment and realized by the brightness of the sun shining through my bedroom curtains that I had overslept. In spite of all the Lord's blessings, the counseling at the church, the times of joy and peace, and the support of other believers, I still struggled with periodic depression. I was constantly exhausted from the struggle to rise above it. I also suffered from insomnia, and after tossing and turning for hours I would finally fall into a deep sleep toward morning. When I woke up, I felt as if I hadn't slept at all.

"Church starts in twenty minutes," I groaned to myself. "There's no time to wash my hair or put on makeup. I'll just have to sneak in and hope no one I know sees me."

I quickly dressed without a shower—which I never do—ran a comb through my hair, grabbed my Bible, and rushed to the car. Sunday morning church was my lifeline. Missing it was absolutely out of the question no matter what my condition was. And I was able to drive there myself now.

I pulled into the parking lot, jumped out of my car, and ran to the church entrance, where I bumped into Terry and her friend Paul. As we greeted one another, they turned and waved excitedly to someone driving into the parking lot.

"That's Michael Omartian. He's coming to this church for the first time," Paul explained.

"Great!" I said, trying to cover my alarm and kicking myself for not at least putting blusher on my cheeks. I wanted to escape before he saw me looking so awful, but it was too late. Michael was out of his car and over to us in what felt like an instant.

"Michael, look who's here. It's Stormie!" Paul said.

"Hi, Michael." I tried to sound joyful. "How have you been?"

"Good," he said, nodding. He looked wonderful. I immediately excused myself and hurried into the church alone. I couldn't bear to sit next to them in my disheveled state.

As soon as the service began, I started to cry and didn't stop until it ended. I don't know what the people sitting around me thought, and Pastor Jack must have wondered what effect his message was having on me that morning. All I could think of was how I had blown everything. I could see now that when Michael first came into my life, God had provided him as an opportunity for me to make the right decision. He had told me the truth about the Lord, and I had been attracted to God's light in him but had resisted it. I had my chance, and as was typical I'd made the wrong choice. Now it was too late.

*Oh, God, I've messed up everything. These past twenty-nine years have been a total waste, but I surrender my life to You. Don't let me ever be in the wrong place again,* I prayed.

Until this moment I had only *received His* life. Now I *gave Him mine.* As I viewed the failure and rubble of my past, I knew I couldn't navigate on my own anymore. I wanted God to take my life and do with it what He wanted. He would certainly do a better job than I had done.

After church there was no way I could slip out unnoticed. Michael stopped me at the door and mentioned that he had just bought a new car the day before. "Would you like to go for a ride?"

"Great," I said, again beating up myself for not at least putting on some lipstick or eye makeup before I left home.

During our short drive we caught up on the past two years.

"You've done well, Michael," I said, smiling. "I hear you're the hot new piano player in town. You remember that I said you would be, right?"

He laughed. Then his countenance became solemn. "I hear you're divorced."

I looked down and nodded. "It's okay if *you* want to say 'I told you so.'"

"I feel that I failed you by not pressing the reality of Jesus into your life, Stormie. If I'd tried harder, I may have helped you understand. If you had received Him then, none of this would have happened."

"I can't tell you how many times I wished you had done that, but it's too late now. That's all in the past, and the important thing is that I know Him today. Please don't blame yourself. It was what I saw in your life that attracted me to Jesus in the first place. I saw Him in you and Terry and later Pastor Jack. I just didn't know what it was at the time."

I was shocked when he suggested that we meet and talk again the following weekend. "Surely You have blinded this man, God," I said out loud on the way home in my car. "Or else he feels sorry for me. I couldn't look worse than I do today. Lord, please don't let me make another mistake. If I shouldn't be with Michael, I'm willing to not see him again." I was serious about that, and it was further evidence that my prayer earlier that morning in church was sincere.

I felt no uneasiness about seeing Michael the following weekend, so when Saturday night came I washed my hair, carefully styled it, and put on my makeup with the hand of an artist. When he met me at my front door, he must have wondered if I was the same woman he had seen the previous Sunday. We went out to dinner that night and saw each other every weekend after that over the next few months. When we made arrangements to go out to dinner *during* the week, I knew it was serious.

I especially loved going to church with Michael on Sunday mornings. After the service, we would go out for lunch and talk about the teachings from the Bible and what the Lord was doing in our lives each week. Praying together drew us closer to each other as we continued to learn about God's ways and discover His plans for our lives.

After about a year of dating, Michael asked me to marry him. I didn't have to ask him for time to think it over, for I'd already prayed about the possibility in-depth. "God, let Your perfect will be done concerning our relationship," I'd prayed day after day of our entire season of getting to know one another.

"Michael, there's something I need to tell you," I said bravely. "There are things I've done that I've never told anyone." I proceeded to confess everything of my past to him, for I wanted this to be a relationship of total honesty, no matter the risk. When I finished, his look of concern turned to a grin and he said, "That's it?"

"Isn't that enough?" I asked incredulously.

But he wasn't put off by any of it.

⁂

Once we were married, there were many problems to work through. Fortunately, the problems were not between us—*yet*—but individually we were dealing with scars of the past, and being married caused those things to surface.

Michael was never abused as a child. He had a wonderful family. But his mother, whom I loved from the time I first met her, told me herself that she had been a domineering woman with extremely high expectations to which Michael felt he could never live up. She told me she had made mistakes as a mother.

"I was way too hard on him as a child," she tenderly confessed to me one afternoon. Her big, expressive brown eyes were filled with hurt and remorse. They conveyed the guilt that torments any parent upon realizing that he or she has made mistakes with a child. "He feels he can never be good enough, and it's my fault." She sighed heavily.

"Michael is a good man and a faithful husband," I said to encourage her. "The problems of the past are definitely a reality, but he's getting over them, and God is using them to show Himself strong in Michael's life. Please don't feel bad. It's all being healed. Really."

She was somewhat comforted but still concerned.

The difference between Michael and me was that he suffered from feelings of never living up to what was expected of him, while I suffered from the belief that no one ever expected anything of me. Part of me always felt like a misfit that should never have been born. Fortunately, the love that Michael and I had for each other provided a strong bond that laid the groundwork for the healing that was to come.

I gradually discovered that while receiving Jesus as my personal Savior and being born into the kingdom of God was instant, allowing Him to become *Lord* over my life was a process. I let Him have more and more of my life as I went along, but each time I thought I had given Him my *all*, I discovered I had only given all I could. If I wanted to live in peace, enjoying the full measure of God's blessing, I had to obey God's Word with an attitude of heart that says, "Show me what to do, Lord, and help me to do it."

I had always written songs, but now my song lyrics were about the Lord. I could barely write them down fast enough as they came quickly to mind. Even the thrill of hearing these songs recorded by Christian artists, and knowing that God was using them for His purpose, didn't erase the feeling that I was unworthy of success. What would it take to ever feel any differently?

I spoke to Diana on the phone at least once a week. She was the best friend I'd ever had, and I felt badly that she was still stuck in her occult practices, as I had been. I prayed for her every day to know that joy I'd found. I knew she was becoming more and more depressed, but one day I was surprised to learn that she was now agoraphobic. She couldn't leave her house even to go to the grocery store. One night I talked to her in-depth about Jesus again, and she received Him over the phone. I asked her to go to church with me on Sunday morning, and she did. She cried all the way through the service the way I had in the beginning.

From then on, Diana couldn't stay away from the church. She soaked up the Bible like a sponge. Eventually, when her husband saw the amazing changes in her, not the least of which was the healing of the agoraphobia that had plagued her, he started attending too and also received the Lord. Diana and I prayed together over the phone about three times a week. Our prayers together were a godsend to us both.

Though such good things as these were happening, I continued to struggle with depression. And, oddly enough, it seemed to be growing in intensity.

Every morning when I woke up, my thoughts were still plagued with plans for suicide, like a bad habit I couldn't break. I wasn't shy about asking for prayer at church, but even then the depression only let up a little and never completely went away.

I couldn't understand why I had the gift of eternal life and total forgiveness from Jesus, a loving pastor who taught me much about God and the Bible, a supportive husband and enough financial security to no longer feel desperate to work in order to survive, and yet I still felt as if I had nothing to live for. What was the matter with me? Was a part of me missing, just like my mother? I still feared that I would end up crazy like her. If I had so much to be happy about and yet remained depressed, if I had everything to live for and was still suicidal, then what hope was there for me? If Jesus was the answer to my every need and He couldn't help me with this, then who could?

As the suicidal feelings increased, Michael urged me to call the church counseling office again. I was embarrassed at the frequency with which I made appointments there, but the staff didn't seem discouraged by that. They ushered me into the assistant pastor's office and I told him about the length and severity of my depression, plus the suicidal feelings that weren't letting up.

He thought a moment, and then he said, "I think you'd better see Mary Anne."

Mary Anne turned out to be a pastor's wife and a member of the regular biblical counseling staff at the church. She was steeped in the Word of God and had great faith to pray for and see people set free from emotional pain. She was highly knowledgeable about my kind of problem and would prove to be the most powerful instrument of God's liberation I ever met.

I entered her office and sat in the chair across the desk from her. She looked up from her papers and gave me a big smile. She had a beautiful face full of intelligence, understanding, and warmth, and I felt comfortable confessing my problems and past to her. She listened for a long time, nodding thoughtfully and seeming not the least bit shocked by anything I said.

"You need deliverance, Stormie," she stated matter-of-factly when I had finished talking. "Do you know what deliverance is?"

I shook my head. I had heard the term but didn't really understand it.

"Don't let the word 'deliverance' frighten you. It's a process of becoming everything God made you to be. Deliverance removes all the past brokenness and bondage from a person's life so that the real *you* can come forth. A lot of people are afraid of deliverance because they think it will change them. But deliverance doesn't *change* you; it *releases* you.

"I'm talking about oppression and not possession," she continued. "There are spirits that attach themselves to you. They can come into anyone's life through the work of the devil, who has been allowed to influence our lives through our own sin. Our responsibility is to pray for freedom from any oppression tormenting you, whether fear or suicidal thoughts or whatever. Deliverance is like salvation in that we don't earn it. It's God's gift to us. But Second Corinthians says that Jesus will *continue* to deliver you.

"I think we should fast and pray and meet again next week to see what God wants to do for you," she continued. "Certain deliverance will not happen in your life except by prayer and fasting."

"Fasting?" I gulped.

I'd heard about fasting from the pastor's teachings. In fact, the whole church was supposed to fast every Wednesday. I guess I thought Pastor Jack was speaking to the church staff, the elders, and the super spiritual. Surely he wasn't talking to me.

"Yes, there is a certain kind of release that will not happen in your life without prayer and fasting," Mary Anne explained. "It's an act of denying yourself and positioning God as everything to you. Isaiah says that fasting is designed to loose the bonds of wickedness, undo heavy burdens, set the oppressed free, and break every yoke."

"Fasting…of course," I said hesitantly, unwilling to reveal my true feelings of concern that I might die in the night if I went to bed without dinner. "How long?" I asked, holding my breath.

"You should stop eating Sunday, and I will see you Wednesday morning at ten," she said confidently.

"Do I just drink water during this time?"

"Yes, water. You don't have any physical problem that would prohibit you from doing that, do you?"

"Oh, no," I answered, trying to think of something.

"Now, during that time you must be much in prayer. Ask God to bring to your mind every sin you've committed, every practice you've been involved with, and list them all on paper. Bring it with you next week."

*I'll be writing day and night,* I thought to myself in horror. "What are you going to do with the paper?" I asked, trying to mask my concern.

"When you've confessed it all and we've prayed, you'll tear it up and throw it away."

"Good," I said with such relief that she gave me her heartwarming laugh at my response.

I left Mary Anne's office feeling hopeful that God was going to do something for me. The fast actually seemed like an adventure, and I was glad I was being forced to do it.

The first days of the fast brought no problems. I worked on my list of failures and drank water every time I felt a hunger pang. On Wednesday morning, as I was getting ready for my appointment with Mary Anne, she telephoned to say she was sick and needed to postpone our meeting for one week. Instantly, my hopes were dashed to the ground. I could hear the congestion in her lungs, and she could barely talk. She was apologetic, and of course I understood. But instead of seeing this as the enemy's attack upon her body, I believed the lie of the enemy that there wouldn't be any liberation for me.

"It's never going to happen," I heard the voice in my head say. "You've had these depressions for at least twenty years and it will never be any different. You were stupid to hope otherwise."

During the week that followed, my depression became so bad that when Michael wasn't home I lay in bed for hours from sheer exhaustion. Mary Anne instructed me to fast again, just as we had the previous week. Although I had lost hope of anything being accomplished through it, I fasted anyway. I would do what she said and let her discover for herself that nothing was going to change.

On the morning of the third day *of the second fast* I wearily got out of bed and dressed, half expecting the phone to ring and the appointment to be canceled. But no one called. Just before I left, Michael and I prayed that God would work a miracle.

Once I was in Mary Anne's office, we got down to the issues immediately. First of all, she had me renounce all my occult involvement, specifically naming each type of practice. "'Let your astrologers come forward,'" she read from the Bible, "'those stargazers who make predictions month by month, let them save you from what is coming upon you.'"[1] She searched for another passage and continued reading. "'There shall not be found among you anyone who…practices witchcraft…or a sorcerer…or a medium…or one who calls upon the dead. For all who do these things are an abomination to the Lord.'"[2]

What the Bible said about the occult was pretty clear. If you are aligned with it, you cannot be aligned with God. I remember Pastor Jack saying, "The occult is real in its power, but wrong in its source. It derives its power from the realm of darkness."

At first I didn't want to believe that these things were wrong. I had always thought of them as a way of getting closer to God. But I believed that the Bible was God's Word, and if God said these things were wrong, I was willing to give up my involvement with them. Yet somehow, in my lack of complete spiritual awakening, I had never thought to *verbally* break the ties I had established with the realm of darkness. I thought that to just stop practicing these things was enough. But I was wrong. I had been aligned with evil, and I had never thought to identify with and break its powerful hold over my life. When Mary Anne read those Scriptures, I knew that this was exactly what I had to do. She instructed me to renounce each practice specifically, and so I did.

When I was finished, Mary Anne prayed over me to be free of all my past occult practices, false religions, and any alignments with the realm of darkness.

Next I took my list of failures and presented them before the Lord. I confessed them all as sin and asked for God's forgiveness. Then Mary Anne instructed me to confess my unforgiveness. "God, I confess my unforgiveness toward my mother. I forgive her for everything she did to me. I forgive her for not loving me. Help me to forgive her completely."

I began to cry, partly because of the relief of being free from the heavy load of failure, guilt, and unforgiveness I had carried so long. I felt the gentle, healing presence of the Holy Spirit around me.

Mary Anne called another pastor's wife into the room to pray alongside her for this last part. While I sat in a chair, they put their hands on my head and worshipped God for many minutes. I kept my eyes closed and felt as if the roof on the small room was being raised with the joy of their praise.

One by one they addressed spirits that had tormented me or had an oppressive hold on my life. Spirits of futility, despair, fear, and rejection were mentioned, as were spirits of suicide and torment. I was not demon possessed, but these spirits had oppressed me at points in my life where I had given them place through my disobedience to God's ways. As they prayed, I felt the physical manifestation of my depression leave, like an enormous burden lifted off my shoulders and chest. What had seemed like a light at the end of the long, dark tunnel of my life became so bright it almost made me want to cover my eyes. *Was it the absence of darkness or the presence of light?* I wondered. *Both*, I decided. *But will the darkness come back by morning? If it does, I'll just come back and see Mary Anne.*

When Mary Anne felt that the oppression was finally broken, she relaxed her grip on my head and rested her hands on my shoulders. She began to speak, not in the powerful voice of authority that she used to pray regarding the oppression I had battled, but in a soft, almost-angelic tone of a prophetic message from God that would change my life forever.

"My daughter, you have been locked in a closet all your life. First physically and then emotionally, but *I* have the keys. *I* have the keys." The voice was Mary Anne's, but I knew the message was from the Lord. Jesus has the keys to unlock the places in me where I had been held prisoner all my life.

"I have set you free, but I am giving the keys to you," the word continued. "Whenever you feel the enemy trying to lock you up again, use the keys I have given you.

"God has also given me a Scripture in Isaiah for you," Mary Anne said as she turned to her Bible lying open on her desk. " 'Speak comfort to Jerusalem, and cry out to her, that her warfare is ended, that her iniquity is pardoned; for she has received from the LORD's hand double for all her sins.'"[3]

Looking up at me she said, "I know the Lord told me to give you that Scripture, but I'm not sure what the words 'double for all her sins' means for you."

"I know exactly what it means," I assured her. "I have always felt that I paid double for everything I've ever done wrong. I've always believed that life has been twice as painful and difficult for me than for anyone else. God is saying I must not think that way anymore. The miserable times are finished and the consequences of my sins have been paid."

It was over and I was drained. With a big, loving smile, Mary Anne gave me a warm hug and said, "God moved in your behalf today, Stormie. You're going to feel like a new person."

"I already do!" I felt as if a thousand pounds of deadweight had been lifted off of me. I felt new.

"I know this may seem like a strange question," I continued, "but do you think I should change my name? As a child I used to hate being teased about it, and even though now it has proven to be a name that people remember, I've always wanted to have a normal name. As long as I'm a new person, should I have a new name?"

Mary Anne replied immediately, "No, I believe you are supposed to keep your name and let it be a testimony to the work that God has done in you. You've come out of a stormy childhood, but God has calmed the tempests in your life. Whenever someone questions you about your name, let that be your opportunity to share about God's goodness."

I knew she had again given me a word from God, so I laid that issue to rest once and for all. I thanked the two powerful prayer warriors and hugged them goodbye.

"Walk in all the freedom God has given you," Mary Anne instructed me. "Read your Bible and pray every day, and attend church as often as you can. This will give you a strong armor of protection from the enemy, who will attempt to steal back this territory in your life that has been taken away from him. It's not that what God accomplished in you can easily be undone, but the enemy could certainly undermine it by causing you to have doubt and fear again. Do not allow it."

I left her office dazed and almost numb. As I drove home, I tried to remember all that happened. I had gone there without much hope. I believed that God *could* do something, but I didn't know whether He *would* do it for me. Although I had sensed His presence in the whole process, what it would all mean in my life I still didn't know. And what were the keys that God was talking about? I still wondered if all that anxiety and depression would come back in the morning.

Michael was gone when I arrived home. I ate some fruit—my first food in three days—and went to bed. A few hours later my husband came home and woke me up from a sound sleep.

"Tell me what happened with Mary Anne." His voice reflected the concern on his face. This had been a draining time for him too, but my own emotional paralysis had blinded me to the effect of it on him until now.

Halfway through the story he interrupted me: "Your eyes look totally different. They're peaceful, not fearful or worried."

The next morning I awoke without any feelings of depression whatever. No thoughts of suicide, no heaviness in my chest, no fearful anticipation of the future, no anxiety. I waited all day for them to return, but they didn't. Day after day it was the same.

I never again experienced those paralyzing feelings. I am not saying I was never depressed again, because depressing things happen in life. But depression never controlled me from that time on.

I learned about the keys. If I began to feel depressed about something, I could go to God and use the keys He had given me to rise above it.

I remembered the words of Jesus: "The people who sat in darkness have seen a great light, and upon those who sat in the...shadow of death Light has dawned." [4]

*That was me. I've been living in the shadow of death. I've felt it for years and thought I could never escape it. That was the big lie I had accepted. But now the Lord Jesus—the One True Light—had dawned on me and I will never be the same. I feel it. I know it.*

I realized many people suffered with depression due to a chemical imbalance and needed medical treatment to balance that out. I carefully made that distinction when talking to others about what happened to me. I didn't say God couldn't heal them too, but I didn't want people to go off medicine they needed until they and their doctor knew they were ready. "Taking medicine does not indicate a lack of faith as some would suggest," I assured them. "God gives us doctors and medicine too."

I thought every day about what had happened to me. I had gone into that counseling office knowing Jesus as Savior, but I came out knowing Him also as my Deliverer. I saw the power of prayer and fasting. I wondered, *What else does God want to do in my life and in the lives of others?*

# 12

# Keys to Unlocking the Kingdom

After my time of deliverance, I spent the rest of the year learning what the keys were that God had given me. I knew that Jesus held the keys to life, and by receiving Him and being born again, the doorway to life after death had been opened for me.

He also completely unlocked the door of my emotional closet that day in the counseling office with Mary Anne. Now I found that the significance of the keys extended far beyond that. If I wanted to experience more life in *this* life, there were keys I needed to use in order to unlock doors on a daily basis—the doors to peace, wholeness, fulfillment, love, abundance, growth, ongoing deliverance, fruitfulness, restoration, purpose, and total wholeness.

One such key was spending time daily in *God's Word* and letting it be inscribed on my heart and in my mind so that it shaped my actions and thoughts. I had no trouble believing that the Bible was God's Word, because after I received Jesus the words practically leaped off the pages, teeming with life when I read it. I developed a hunger for more and more of God's truth in order to feed and fortify the places in my spirit and personality that were long starved or severely undernourished. I memorized certain verses and spoke them out loud when I needed to cut through the dark times of my life with power.

I discovered that for me to get through a day successfully, I needed to read the Bible first thing every morning. It set my mind on the right path from the beginning and gave me a solid foundation on which to build my day. Anytime I was tempted to fall back into the old habit of thinking of myself as a failure or feeling fearful and depressed, I read the Bible until I could feel my attitude reverse and my mind fill with peace.

*The key of God's Word* was also spiritual ammunition to stand against whatever was opposing me. It helped me understand the authority and power given to me through what Jesus accomplished. I combatted lies with truth. When I became fearful and heard a voice in my head saying, "You're no good. You don't deserve to be alive. You're going to end up mentally ill just like your mother," I would speak out loud the Scripture that says, "God has not given us a spirit of fear, but of power and of love and of a sound mind."[1] I'd repeat that over and over with conviction until the fear was gone.

I recognized these thoughts as lies from the realm of darkness—from the enemy—and not in line with God's truth. Lying thoughts had no power now that the father of lies had no hold on me. My heavenly Father helped me to see the truth and stand strong in it.

*The key of prayer* was a big one for me. King David's words, "Early will I seek thee,"[2] resounded in my mind, and I knew I needed to be up early every morning spending time talking with God. I learned that when I took every concern to Him and listened for His guidance, it led to a more peaceful and productive day—a day that was no longer left to chance. I discovered the power that was unleashed when praying in Jesus' name. And I was just tapping the surface.

*The key of confession* was also powerful to unlock the benefits of living in the kingdom of God's light after walking out of the realm of darkness. I confessed everything in my heart that was sin. I used to think that sin meant smoking, drinking, drugs, and sexual immorality, and because I was no longer involved with any of these, and I hadn't murdered anyone or robbed a liquor store, I was exempt from sinner status. How wrong I was! I discovered that "sin" was an old archery term meaning "to miss the bull's-eye." Anything other than direct center was sin. That realization opened up a whole new world for me. Anything less than God's *perfect will* for my life was sin.

In that light, I had plenty to confess. From my critical attitude to doubt, self-hatred, white lies, and selfishness, there were many things I was doing that I never even realized were wrong. I prayed as King David in the Bible did, "'Create in me a clean heart, O God, and renew a steadfast spirit within me.' [3] Lord, show me my 'secret sins' and cleanse me from all of it." [4] God always quickly answered that prayer.

I learned that the rage I had inside me from my childhood was sin, even though it began when I was too young to understand it, and even though there was a good reason for it. Sin is never justified, no matter who commits it or what age they are. God never approves of sin, but He does make provision for it through receiving Jesus. And the key to experiencing that provision is confession. Once we receive Jesus, we are responsible to live His way. When we don't, we are supposed to use our confession key and repent of it. When I didn't do that, I got tied up in guilt and was miserable.

*The key of forgiveness*—both receiving it from Him and extending it to others—was also extremely important. One of the most persistent sins I had to confess was unforgiveness toward my mother. I had to deal with this on a daily basis. I'd confessed my unforgiveness toward her in the counseling office and thought I had taken care of the matter until the very next time I saw her. Then the old feelings of resentment, frustration, bitterness, and anger came rushing forth like a flood, and along with them their partners—defeat, discouragement, and sadness.

"God, I forgive my mother completely," I confessed daily whether I felt like it or not. I knew without a doubt that harboring unforgiveness would keep me from the wholeness and blessings God had for me, and I was convinced it would also make me physically sick. I could never be completely whole as long as I had any unforgiveness in me. I had to keep working on that. But it helped to understand that *forgiveness doesn't make the other person right, it makes you free*. And we have to get free, because we can never move into all God has for us if we don't.

God answered my prayers about forgiving my mother, because my forgiveness of her grew in my heart to such a point that I was eventually able to see her as God made her to be and not the way she was. I saw how the traumas of her life had shaped her, and how she—as I had been—was a victim of her past. Only she never found the way out. Every time I pictured the 11-year-old girl who lost her mother and felt responsible for her death, believing that life and God had deserted her, I felt deep sadness for her. Instead of hating her, I felt sorry and began praying for her healing.

I read up on the subject of mental illness and understood that my mother's brain did not function like the brain of a normal person. I had known that long before, but I still always blamed her for it. Now I saw that she really couldn't help herself. Because of her illness, she was at the mercy of disassociated, unorganized thinking patterns that made no sense. Her illogical and inappropriate behavior, like laughing when I was hurt or becoming enraged when I cleaned my room, were viewed by experts on the subject as "normal" for someone in her condition. There was a major short circuit somewhere. Everything she imagined was completely real to her, and common to those with the same illness. Her mind simply could not sort things through clearly. I felt pity for her and regretted all the times I had been completely insensitive in my response toward her. I now had respect for how well she navigated life considering all she had going against her.

My forgiveness toward her allowed me to recall good memories of her that I hadn't even realized were there. I flashed back to my mother making pancakes for me when I was three, and giving me my first and only birthday party when I was nine. And on my twelfth birthday, when I thought no one had remembered, she gave me a turquoise wool suit she found in a store.

At Christmas she always cooked dinner, made popcorn balls, and bought small gifts for the family. I could see now that she had tried hard to make the season something special, even though it must have been terribly difficult for her. Every part of life must have put tremendous pressure on her, but I never saw *her* misery before—only *mine*.

I had forgotten these events because immediately after each one she always did something horrible and painful that canceled out any good that had been accomplished. But now, because I was forgiving the cruel acts, it was possible to see the kind ones.

I did have a major setback every time I saw my mother in person, however, because even though I became more forgiving of her, her hatred toward me increased along with the progression of her mental illness. I depended on God to help me through each encounter. Eventually, though, I just couldn't be with her anymore and I called Mary Anne. She instructed me to honor her from afar and not continue allowing her to abuse me. So I did that by writing her uplifting cards and letters and sending her many gifts I knew she wanted and needed.

*The key of saying yes to God* was a matter of trusting Him in all things. Every time I thought I had all my problems solved, I found myself at another crossroads, where God asked me for a deeper commitment to Him. He asked me to surrender my dreams about becoming someone important. The things I accomplished in my career were always about placing my identity in those accomplishments, but God wanted my identity to be in *Him*. He spoke to my heart saying, "Whether you accomplish anything or not—even if you are rejected in the world's eyes—you are valuable to Me." It brought great comfort.

So in God's cleanup program, all excess baggage had to be eliminated, the most major of which was *self*. All my desires to be noticed, to be somebody, to do something great, had to be given up to the Lord. My dreams had to be *His* dreams, the ones *He* placed in my heart. They couldn't be the ones I thought I should have.

"Okay, Lord," I finally said with much reluctance. "I will no longer regard not being a success in the world's eyes as a failure." I stopped doing all TV shows and studio singing. I did nothing but go to church, take care of my home and husband, and watch all my dreams come crashing down as a part of me died a little every day. The death process was long and painful.

Through it all God taught me that I had to let everything go, depend totally on Him, and live His way. I read where Jesus said, "If anyone loves Me, he will keep My word; and My Father will love him, and We will come to him and make Our home with him."[5] I recognized then that there was a clear link between my obedience and enjoying the presence of God in greater measure. His presence was light and life to me, and I wasn't about to jeopardize that by having any connection with the realm of darkness.

I saw how sin results in death, and it doesn't get any darker than that. The more I obeyed God and lived His way, the more I moved into the light of His blessings. But it wasn't easy facing who I was in order to become who God made me to be. I had to deliberately step out of darkness and choose every day to live in His light.

Stormie, 18 months old.

Stormie, 6 months old, with her mother
outside their house.

Stormie, 4 years old.

Stormie, 6 years old, on the first day of school, getting
on the van after nearly dying of diphtheria.

Stormie, 7 years old, shopping with her mother.

Stormie's mother and father.

Stormie, on the far right, working on television with
Glen Campbell and the other three singers.

Stormie, about 22 years old, working in theater in L.A.

Stormie, working in television.

Stormie and Michael, newly married.

Stormie and Michael collaborating on Michael's *White Horse* album.

Stormie reading bedtime stories to Christopher, age 6, and Amanda, age 2.

Christopher, age 8, and Amanda, age 4.

Christopher, age 18.

Amanda, early 20s.

Christopher and Paige are married.

Amanda and Dallas are married.

The back cover photo for some of Stormie's books.

Michael, before the move to Tennessee.

Michael and Stormie at home.

Michael and Stormie, working on songs for a project.

Paige, Scarlett, and Christopher together for their first Christmas.

Scarlett Grace, our first grandchild, about a month old.

"Here I am in the hospital, receiving the best Mother's Day gift only minutes after she was born. It doesn't get any better than that."

# 13

# Stepping Out of Darkness

I thought about how many times in my past—even after I became a believer—I had begged God to do what *I* wanted Him to do, yet I never bothered to find out what *He* wanted *me* to do. How often had I been mad at God for not giving me what I desired, yet it never entered my mind to find out what *He* desired from me?

I came across the Scripture "Anyone who competes as an athlete does not receive the victor's crown except by competing according to the rules."[1] How foolish I was to demand that God let me win at the game of life while I refused to play by His rules! The more committed I became to living God's way, the more I saw that the way I had been living wasn't pleasing to Him. God had accepted me the way I was, but He wasn't about to leave me that way. One by one, He surfaced things in me that needed to be gone.

Early one morning I came across the Scripture, "Do not bring a detestable thing into your house or you, like it, will be set apart for destruction."[2] I shuddered and knew that my housecleaning day had arrived. I went on a search-and-destroy mission of any "detestable thing" I had brought into our home. I went through every inch of our house and threw out whatever was not of God or was even questionable in nature. Sixty or seventy expensive hardcover books on different areas of the occult and Eastern religions went into the trash, along with paintings, sculptures, wall hangings, hand-painted trays, miscellaneous artifacts—anything that exalted other gods. I thought for a moment about giving those things to some of my old friends who were still into those practices, but I came to my senses and realized how totally wrong it was to lead someone deeper into the darkness from which I was escaping. So I destroyed them all by ripping them apart and throwing them in the trash. It took days.

I gave away things that were a reminder of my first marriage, an old boyfriend, or an unhappy time in my life, if they could be put to good use by other people who had no negative ties to them the way I did.

Into the trash went tapes and records that had ungodly lyrics on them. Out went the novels that exalted lifestyles and thinking patterns that were opposed to God's ways. This all might have sounded like a witch hunt to anyone who didn't understand, but it wasn't. It was a sound-minded decision to separate myself from anything that separated me from God. I had experienced enough of God's presence and blessings to know that I wanted *all* He had for me. When I finished this housecleaning, I felt light, clean, and joyful.

I decided that since my house and I had been born again, it was time that my wardrobe was too. I threw out tight pants, revealing sweaters, low-cut dresses, and sexy outfits that were not befitting a daughter of the God of the universe. I marveled that I had worn these things to church and didn't once receive stares of condemnation from Pastor Jack or Anna, his wife. They never made me feel as if I were less than anyone else, although I knew I had certainly given them reason to think that by my wardrobe alone. When I showed up late for church in my tight jeans and skimpy T-shirt, with no makeup and unstyled hair, they always welcomed me as if I were the guest speaker. They accepted me as God accepted me—the way I was. And their love was a major part of my healing. But they, like God, were committed to seeing me move on in the Lord. And they, like God, did it with love and not condemnation.

As I discarded all of these things, I knew I had to do the same with certain habits and relationships. I stopped watching TV shows that exalted godless activity and became selective about what movies I went to see. Filling my mind with violence, foul language, disrespectful use of God's name, and other people's sex acts didn't make me feel good in my spirit, and I knew it didn't bless God's Spirit in me either. The Bible said I was the temple of the Holy Spirit of God, so how could I enjoy the fullness of His presence if He was being crowded out by all that was opposed to Him and His ways? As I separated myself from these things, I felt more and more fulfilled and happy. I experienced greater spiritual light in my life.

I gradually realized that certain of my unbelieving friends were a bad influence on me. They had a drawing power in them that pulled me away from the things of God and back into my old life. Even though I cared for these people, I knew the relationships had to go. My method for handling those particular friendships was quite simple. All I had to do was tell them about my new life in Jesus and invite them to share it. The ones who responded remained as friends, and those who didn't were gone in a flash.

Some spiritual housecleaning happened without my doing anything. One day I woke up and realized that my fear of knives was gone. I don't know how it happened, but I assumed it was because of God's promise in the Bible says, "Perfect love drives out fear." [3] It also says that "if anyone obeys his word, love for God is truly made complete in them." [4] There is a definite connection between *obedience* and *receiving God's love*. Through my *obedience* I was able to *receive* more of God's love, and God's love, in turn, crowded out my fears and brought great healing.

Through my steps of obedience I began to see things more clearly. I identified the dark spirits of the occult I had aligned myself with as being of the same spirit that inspired the people involved in the Sharon Tate murders. I had *felt* aligned with that evil because I *was* aligned in the spirit realm with a spirit of evil.

For the first time I saw abortion for what it was—the taking of a human life. What had never entered my mind before now came in with full conviction. I recalled my feeble bargain with God before the first abortion: "God, please get me through this and I'll be good." What a joke! I didn't even know what good was, and even if I had, there was no way I could accomplish it without the power of Jesus and His Holy Spirit in me.

With each of the two abortions, I firmly believed that the baby's soul and spirit entered his body only at the time of birth. It was a common theory I had been told back then, and it never occurred to me that I was taking the life of a person. "It's not a human being," I reasoned, "but just a mass of cells." Because I believed that, I had little conscious guilt about what I had done. That, however, didn't make it any less wrong or the consequences any less shattering. Even though I had confessed my wrongdoing earlier and been released from the consequences of it, I still lacked a full understanding of how deeply I had violated God's ways.

As I read the Scriptures, it became clear that God's purposes and plans for those individuals were established from the moment of conception. Whether it was legal or not, whether I felt guilt or not, the facts were the same: I had destroyed two lives in which God had placed gifts, talents, and purpose. Those deaths manifested themselves in my own life as I felt myself dying inside a little more each day. I never made the connection at the time. I thought I was saving my life by having the abortions when actually I was losing it.

As I grew more knowledgeable of God's ways and more obedient to His rules, I could see that every rule and commandment was established by God for *our* benefit. It wasn't to make us miserable and keep us from having fun, but to bring us to the greatest level of fulfillment and purpose. And all because He loves us.

Every new step of obedience I took also brought increased physical health as well. Having hope for my future helped me to take better care of my body, which I now recognized as the temple of God's Spirit.

The more I walked in obedience to God, the more wholeness I enjoyed. It took an attitude of a heart that says "I love You and Your laws, Lord. And I *choose* to walk Your way. Holy Spirit, *enable* me to do what is right."

God is so good that He freely gives us His love, His presence, His healing, His deliverance, and His emotional restoration to all who are willing to step out of darkness and play by the rules He has established. But walking in the light of God's will doesn't mean the road will always be easy. In fact, I have never found life easy. There has been one challenge after another, even as a believer. But I found that when I walk through those times with God, He brings good out of them.

# 14

# The Unexpected Abuser

I never wanted children. It wasn't that I didn't like them. It's just that my goal was to pull myself up out of poverty, and I knew I would have to do that by myself, for there would never be anyone to help me. Poverty is not as much fun as certain politicians try to make it out to be. "Here, take this pittance and you will be free to follow your dream," they say. I noticed that these purveyors of poverty do not take their own advice. They get rich proclaiming a lie. Poverty is not liberty. It is shackles and imprisonment. I knew that from experience, and I decided to educate myself and work my way out of it. If I had a child I could never do that, and I wasn't going to bring a child into poverty.

From all the men I had ever known before Michael, there was not one who would or could ever willingly contribute anything to my life that would make it possible for me to stay home and raise a child.

By contrast, when I started dating Michael, it amazed me how generous he was. When we went out to dinner, I didn't have to pay for it. It was never a question in his mind. He paid for it. I couldn't believe it. He was amazingly kind.

Michael and I never discussed having children before we were married. We didn't have any premarital counseling that would have brought this subject up. The reason for that is because the pastor at our church had made it clear to me that he would never marry two people if either one of them had been divorced. That left us with no alternative but to go elsewhere to be married. The pastor years later recanted his position on that and apologized for his attitude about it.

Neither Michael nor I had ever done anything normal like everyone else, and that's because we never had the luxury of *being* normal. We always had to compensate for something else we were dealing with. We had parents who didn't have the slightest idea what our problems were and why, and how we both struggled to be normal but couldn't.

When we were married, we surrendered our lives to the Lord on every level, including whether we would become parents. The first year we weren't interested in children, so we didn't pray about having any. The second year we prayed about that, and God changed our hearts to an unexpected peace. I had a fear of childbirth because my mother's mother had died in childbirth, along with the child. And I'd heard that story over and over countless times as my mother painted a graphic picture of how having a child "ruins your life if it doesn't kill you."

I was shocked when, after Michael and I made the decision to have our first child, that I didn't get pregnant immediately. Judging from my past, I thought conceiving a child would be no problem for me. But when month after month went by, I feared it was punishment for the abortions I'd had. Still not fully understanding God's mercy and grace, I couldn't comprehend a love so great that it reached beyond the confines of my failure and recovered everything that had been lost. Nor could I fathom a God who didn't punish as I deserved. But I began to believe He would not give us peace about having a child and then not give us the ability to do so.

Michael had been in counseling for some time regarding his fear of traveling—agoraphobia—the same as my friend Diana's fear, which she was able to rise above. It wasn't a fear of airplane crashes, but rather an intense anxiety about being away from the security and familiarity of home. It was something he knew he had to get free of, and he was concentrating on that particular problem. So the fact that I wasn't pregnant didn't concern him as much as it did me.

One morning as I was again praying to conceive a child, God spoke clearly to my heart. He said, "You are going to have a son, and he is going to be conceived in Jerusalem."

I shook my head and said, "Would You repeat that please, Lord?"

There was no repeating, but the original words clearly resounded in my head.

*Surely I'm making this up,* I thought. *But then again, why would I make up something as ridiculous as that?* I pondered it off and on for a few weeks and then dismissed it from my mind.

A few months later I came home from a church meeting with a brochure that Pastor Jack had given our Bible study group about a three-week tour he and Anna were taking to the Holy Land. They were asking only 30 people to go with them, so anyone who wanted to go should sign up immediately. I casually remarked to Michael about what fun that would be, and he abruptly said, "Let's do it."

"Do what?" I asked, not at all expecting his next remark.

"Let's go with Pastor Jack and Anna to visit the Holy Land."

"What?" I exclaimed. "You've got to be kidding! You don't like driving to San Diego, let alone taking a plane clear across the world for three weeks. Are you joking?"

He wasn't joking, and over the next few months we readied ourselves for the trip. During the two weeks before our departure, I became quite ill with a lung infection. For a while it appeared as though we wouldn't be able to go, but I recovered enough, just in time, and off we went.

At the beginning of the tour—in Rome and Greece—Michael did fairly well with his travel anxiety, but by the fourth day, in Israel, he was suffering severely. Late one evening he broke down and said, "I just can't make it. Do you mind if we forget the trip and go home?"

"No," I said, concerned. "Do whatever you need to do, but we must call Pastor Jack. We can't leave without telling him."

We hesitated to call because it was near midnight and the tour had an exhausting schedule, but Michael was determined to take the first flight out the next day. Pastor Jack came to our room immediately, talked with Michael for a long time, and then prayed for him to be free of the fear and insecurity that was tormenting him. He put his arms around Michael and held him as a father would a son while Michael sobbed. I witnessed the love of God working through a compassionate pastor and an obedient son, and I saw deliverance and healing happen in my husband because of it.

As a result of that night, we stayed on the tour and there was a total turn-about in Michael. Five days later we finally had a free day in Jerusalem, and because of the intensity of the tour it was the first chance Michael and I had to spend time alone with each other. After that day the hectic schedule resumed. We rose before dawn, went full speed, and fell exhausted into bed at night.

When we arrived at the Sea of Galilee near the end of our tour, I became extremely ill. I was dizzy and nauseated every day, and I couldn't keep any food down. It became progressively worse, and we tried unsuccessfully to get an earlier flight out of Israel back to California. The only solution was to send me on to Tel Aviv to stay in our hotel there and wait for the rest of the group to catch up.

When we finally left Tel Aviv, our plane made an emergency stop in Paris for mechanical reasons. I was taken to the hospital and given a shot to control the nausea and vomiting and to ward off dehydration long enough for me to get back to California. Even so, the ride home was miserable. I was so violently sick that everyone, including me, thought I must have food poisoning.

Being pregnant didn't occur to me because I associated the violent sickness of my first two pregnancies with my own psychological rejection of them. But once we were back in California, I soon found out that I was indeed pregnant and that my extreme illness during pregnancy was a condition called hyper-emesis gravidarum. I was afraid of the violent nausea and pain I felt in my body day and night, afraid that I might die in childbirth like my grandmother, and afraid that my life really was over just like my mother warned.

Mother's reaction to my pregnancy was hard to read. She was more concerned with all the people who were following her. She said the president of the United States was having her watched and that the Communists were trying to kill her because she knew too much. There were times when she seemed so normal and her story sounded so convincing that I wondered, *Wouldn't we*

*feel terrible if what she's been saying is true and all this time none of us believed her?*
But then she would give herself away by saying that Frank Sinatra and the Pope
were conspiring to have her shot. I guess if I were convinced that they were
trying to have *me* shot, I might be more concerned with that than the birth of
my first grandchild. It's hard to say. Anyway, I was disappointed that she didn't
seem to care.

Dad, on the other hand, was very excited and yet also worried. I was so sick
that by the end of four months I had lost 13 pounds. On a body still too thin,
this did not look attractive. Dad was well aware of our family history of serious
pregnancy complications and his concern was evident.

I called Mary Anne about the problem. I knew my fear had to go, and I
thought the nausea and pain might be caused by it. She assured me that I was
not the same as my grandmother or my mother, and that this was also a different time, so I would not be dying in childbirth. She also pointed out that what
my mother taught me on the subject was a reflection of her own feelings and
totally opposite from the Word of God, which says that children are a gift and
a blessing from the Lord. Then she prayed for me to be free from the fear. As
she did, I felt a heaviness lift immediately. Unfortunately, the nausea and the
pain remained.

My obstetrician said nearly the same thing when I questioned him about
whether I could inherit my grandmother's condition. The doctor said, "You
are not your grandmother, Stormie, and this is a different time. We know so
much more today."

When nothing helped my condition, I became increasingly concerned that
I might lose the baby. One evening while crying out to God about it, the words
He had spoken to me nearly six months earlier flooded my memory.

"You are going to have a son, and he is going to be conceived in Jerusalem."

I thought back. Michael and I had been together on that one free day in
Jerusalem. First because of my lung infection, and then because of the hectic
traveling schedule, it was the only possible time I could have conceived. I was
amazed as I put all of the facts together. "God," I said, revealing the magnitude
of my faith, "if this turns out to be a boy, then I'll know I really heard from

You." At that time we couldn't find out the gender of a child before birth except by a procedure that had an element of risk to the baby. We'd decided against it.

When I told Michael all that God had spoken to my heart, he was relieved. Over the next difficult months of the pregnancy, I was sick the entire time and deeply concerned for the health of my child. I hung on to God's words, repeating over and over to myself, "God has ordained this pregnancy, and He will bring forth this child." My husband lost patience with the situation when we prayed every day and yet nothing changed.

Four weeks earlier than planned I suddenly went into heavy labor. The baby was positioned sideways and unable to be born naturally, so I had to have an emergency Cesarean section. We were frightened, but I still kept hearing God's words to me. Just as predicted, a healthy baby boy was born on June 25, 1976—right on Pastor Jack's birthday! Christopher Omartian was immediately our most memorable souvenir of the Holy Land.

Very soon after bringing the baby home from the hospital, old feelings that I thought were dead began to rise up in me. All the rage and hatred I had ever had for my mother returned in full force. I looked at my beautiful boy and thought, "How could anyone treat a precious child the way my mother treated me?"

"God, why am I feeling all this?" I questioned. "Haven't I forgiven her?" I didn't yet realize that when God begins a work, He keeps perfecting it. All of these negative feelings were surfacing because He wanted to take me to a new level of deliverance. I felt that I was going backward and I'd lost the deliverance I had already received, but God's truth was that as long as I was following Him, I would go from "glory to glory" and "strength to strength." [1] It was God's desire to give me more freedom in this area than ever before, and now was the time for me to receive it. What surfaced was something I had no idea resided in me. Only having my own child would fully expose it.

I was determined to be a good mother—in fact, the best mother possible. After all, I was well aware of the pitfalls of bad mothering. *I will never be like my mother,* I convinced myself. *My child will have the best care I can give him.*

One night when Christopher was just a few months old, I couldn't get him to stop crying. Michael was working late and I was alone in the house. I tried feeding him, but that didn't help. I changed his diaper. I put warmer clothes on him, then cooler clothes. I held him and rocked him. I tried everything a mother can do, but it made no difference. He screamed all the more. In the middle of his crying, I was close to crying myself.

The frustration built until I finally snapped and lost control. I slapped my baby on the back, the shoulder, and the head. My heart pounded wildly, my face burned, my eyes were blinded by hot tears, and my breathing became shallow and labored. I was out of control.

The baby screamed even more, and that suddenly became a rejection of me. "My son doesn't love me because I'm not a good mother" was the lie I heard in my head. Because rejection was so foundational for me, it pushed me over the edge.

"Stop crying!" I yelled at him. "Stop crying!"

I realized I was one step away from throwing him across the room. The energy inside me was limitless, and I knew if I yielded to it I could injure him badly—maybe even kill him.

The only alternative was to get away from the baby. I laid him in his crib, ran to my bedroom, and fell on my knees beside the bed. "Lord, help me!" I cried. "There's something horrible in me. You've got to take it away. I don't know what it is. I love my baby more than anything in the world. What's the matter with a mother who hurts the child she loves? Please, whatever is wrong with me, take it away." I sobbed into the bedspread.

I was on my knees before God for nearly an hour. Christopher's screaming subsided when he cried himself to sleep.

Michael came home before the baby woke up again, but I didn't tell him anything. I couldn't. I didn't know what to say. It was too mortifying to even think about it, let alone confess to my husband. When the baby woke up, he seemed totally fine. He acted as if nothing had happened, and so did I.

Four or five days later it happened again—the baby's nonstop crying, my feelings of rejection, something snapping inside me, my emotions going out of control, the desire to beat him and my catching myself in time to put Christopher in the crib, go into my bedroom, fall on my knees before God, and cry to Him for help.

I was flooded with guilt. What kind of mother was I? All my good intentions were melted by the fire of rage that burned within me. Again I stayed on my knees until I felt the intensity of what gripped me lift and the forgiveness of God flood in to wash away my guilt. God's love sustained me in the terrible loneliness I experienced because of the secret I couldn't bear to share.

Over the next few weeks I began to understand some of what was happening and why. The face of an abuser became clearer. All my life I had looked at my situation from the standpoint of one who has been abused. It was shocking to discover that I had all the potential in me to be an *abuser*. It was built in me from childhood. I had seen that violent, out-of-control behavior before—in my mother. I knew it wasn't my child that I hated. It was me. And now I was also able to see that it wasn't *me* that my mother hated; it was herself. My compassion for her grew.

I eventually confessed all of this to my husband, and to my relief he was not horrified. Surprised, yes. But not fearful, repulsed, or rejecting of me in any way. He offered to pray with me anytime I needed it, and added, "You know, I get irritated too when the baby doesn't stop crying."

"It's more than that," I said, trying to make him understand. "In between the times I lose control, I experience what I believe to be normal irritation and frustration. What I'm talking about is different. It's way out of proportion to the offense."

With Michael's support I called Mary Anne and told her the situation. She prayed with me, and we both believed that as long as the baby was safe, I was mature enough in the Lord to work this problem out with God. She told me this wasn't going to be solved through instant deliverance. This was a step-by-step process, a little at a time. And she was right. The healing process was long and slow. I prayed about it nearly every day over the next several years, and what the Lord showed me through it all was how much He loved me.

In the beginning I found it shocking to know that the capability of abusing my child had been hidden in my personality. What I was facing was a little-understood problem at that time. I had always thought of child abusers as scum of the earth, insensitive, uneducated, despicable, low-life types. As I looked at that image of them and then examined myself, I didn't feel that I fit into any of those categories. My husband and I had a music ministry, we had positions of leadership in our church, and we led a prayer and Bible study group that met in our home. No one would ever have imagined I was struggling with this problem.

Was it possible that the common denominator between all abusive parents is that somewhere in their past they were abused too? If so, what about my mother? She wasn't abused as a child. But as I checked further into this, I saw that there were other factors to consider.

People who abuse their children have emotions that have never been fed. A child needs love and affection, and without these the child fails to develop emotionally and becomes crippled in that area. Whether caused by trauma, having love withheld, verbal or physical abuse, or sexual molestation, the emotions have shut off and stopped growing. The body grew because it was fed food and the mind grew because it was stimulated, but the emotions never grew. Down inside every abuser is a child who needs to be loved into wholeness. My mother had not been abused, but through great trauma and tragedy she felt rejected and unloved. Whether it was real or imagined, she still suffered the same consequences.

This gave me increased compassion for abusive parents. Like me, they were caught in a trap. Once started, child abuse is something that can be passed on from generation to generation unless it is stopped. I knew that the power of God was the only power great enough to stop it. Fortunately, in spite of my intense feelings of rejection, I stopped short of child abuse because of the healing I'd already had. Without that I, too, would have been an abusive parent.

I asked God daily to help me raise my son because I knew I couldn't do it on my own. That little boy was the most wonderful gift God had ever given me, and the thought of harming him in any way was too painful to even think about. I prayed, "God, don't let Christopher suffer the way I suffered. Don't let him feel unloved or rejected like I did. Don't let me damage him in any way."

It took several years to be completely healed enough to share my story about that, but when I did share it publicly, I was unprepared for the response. A flood of people had been through similar experiences. I had no idea how great the need for emotional healing was for those who had been abused in childhood and were carrying on the same tradition with their own children. Everywhere I went the response was overwhelming. I received countless letters from people crying out for help who had been victims of the past and were now trapped in their present circumstances with no vision of hope for their future.

"If there is deliverance and healing for me, then it is there for you too," I told them. "You *can* get free of the past and the paralyzing hold it has on you. Things *can* be different. But it can only happen through the power and love of Jesus." The Bible says, "From *the* LORD comes deliverance!"[2] He is the deliverer. He is the healer. Without *Him* we cannot make ourselves completely whole.

"The way it happened for me was by simply spending more and more time in God's presence," I continued to explain. "God asks us to make Him the center of our lives and to continually seek His presence. When we do that, His presence answers our every need. The Bible says, 'The Lord is the Spirit; and where the Spirit of the Lord is, there is liberty.'[3] It also says, 'He will deliver the needy when he cries, the poor also, and him who has no helper.'[4] Whenever I cried out to God about this, He met me in my need. He is there for those without a counselor, without anyone to talk to, without someone else to understand."

Deliverance from child-abusing tendencies took time because I needed to learn a new way of thinking. I had to seek God's presence and stay there long enough for my heart to change. While it's good to seek counseling, I knew I could not live in a counselor's office. I had to become better acquainted with *the Counselor*. I had to let Him love me into wholeness.

My first deliverance from suicidal depression, anxiety, and feelings of worthlessness was instant. Liberation from child-abusing tendencies was a step-by-step process as God's love healed me little by little.

At this time, the church was growing faster than we had room for people. So while a new church was being built, the pastor asked us to be one of a number of couples to hold group meetings in our home once a month on Sunday morning. We started with 18 people. Michael led the worship time on the piano, and he did a short Bible teaching that was prepared for all home group leaders on that day. That allowed home groups to take about 25 percent of the people out of the congregation every week in order to make room for more people in church.

The home groups provided an environment where people could get to know one another and pray together. I led the prayer time and asked anyone who had a prayer request to share it with the rest of us so we could pray about it. To my surprise, *everyone* had a major prayer request and was not reluctant to share it. We had to dismiss at a set time—before we could fit everyone in who needed prayer—so I invited those who wanted to stay afterward for prayer to do so, and many did.

It quickly became apparent that we needed to have a separate night once a month just for prayer. When we scheduled it, about 20 people came to the first meeting. Michael took the men in the den, and I took the women into our bedroom, where we all sat cross-legged in a big circle on our king-sized bed. There was something about that intimate circle in a private room that allowed every woman to open up about her deepest need, struggle, and heartfelt desires. Each one shared things about which none of us would ever have dreamed they were suffering or struggling. I still remember each woman and each prayer request as though it were yesterday. I had seen the power of God move in *my* life in so many powerful ways. Now I saw the power of God move in the lives of these women as well.

Over that year, our home group grew to 75 people, which was a lot of people for our house. But mostly it became a lot of people to pray for one night a month. Eventually, the entire group was too large and had to be divided into smaller groups. We stepped down as home group leaders when we moved to another town. We stayed in the same church and started having prayer groups in our home. We had a prayer group to pray for all of our children. We had another prayer group of couples to pray for our marriages. We had a prayer group to pray over work, careers, and ministries. Later on, I had a group of women that met weekly to pray for our specific needs.

Seeing God answer prayer after prayer in all categories was thrilling. We each learned much about the benefit and power of praying together with others. It was life changing, and bonds were formed that I know will last forever.

Through all of that I saw the amazing power of prayer as we came humbly to God to share our hearts with Him and look to Him to meet our needs. In every prayer time we read God's Word and worshipped Him before we shared our requests and prayed.

Our prayer groups became like a cocoon of safety. We all felt it. Every time we prayed, things happened in the spirit realm, and the realm of darkness was pushed back in each of our lives.

# 15

# Unimagined Miracles

In light of all the restoration God was working in my life, I repeatedly asked Him to heal my mother and restore the relationship between us. However, it seemed that the more I prayed for her, the worse she became.

Dad retired from working, and he and my mother moved to a five-acre farm in central California. It was perfect for him, being a farmer at heart. He loved raising cows and horses and planting a large garden. With no more city stress and pollution, but instead leisurely working outside in the clean air and eating fresh fruits and vegetables from his garden, I could see his life being extended by this way of living.

At first the move appeared to be good for my mother too, but as always, her surge of normality was only temporary. This time she sank into her fantasy world even quicker and deeper than before. Her bitterness and hatred were now all directed toward my father. In her hysterical moments, Dad's method of coping was to calmly walk out of the house and leave her to fight by herself. He was a pacifist at heart. This incensed her so much that one day she picked up a large, dead tree branch, crept up behind him as he was stooped over pulling weeds in the garden, and sent it crashing across his back. She had amazing strength when she was full of rage. Another time, when he was outside on a very cold winter day, she turned on the garden hose and drenched him with icy water.

As her actions became more openly hostile and violent, I became more concerned about Dad. I asked the church to pray about her condition at one of the services. Thousands of people prayed, and I hoped God would answer and my mother would be healed. However, I learned that prayer is not telling God what to do. It's partnering with God to do what He wants. So instead of getting better, she continued to grow worse, this time with a new twist.

It was normal for my mother to sleep all day and prowl the house at night, fighting imaginary enemies. One morning she woke Dad at three in the morning. She had been cooking since midnight, and she had a full meal prepared and the table set for six people. She told Dad that her voices had informed her I was coming for dinner. Now they told her I was lost in town somewhere. She wanted Dad to drive her around to search for me.

He accommodated her as he always did—his peace-at-any-price mode of operation. Anyone else would have told her to go back to bed or had her committed, but not Dad. He put up with her insanity for reasons that only he could understand.

At 4:30 in the morning, I received a call.

"Stormie?" my dad's voice sounded tired.

"Dad? What's wrong?" I asked, awakening quickly.

"Your mother said you were coming for dinner and that you were lost in town. We've been looking for you since three this morning. Are you coming?"

"Of course not, Dad. I'm here in bed."

"I want you to tell your mother so she knows." He handed the phone to her.

"Where are you?" she said gruffly.

"I'm home in bed. Where am I supposed to be?"

"You told me you were coming for dinner." Her anger gained momentum.

We hadn't spoken in weeks and had not seen each other in months. The farm was a four-hour car ride away, so it was not the kind of trip anyone would make just for dinner.

"I never told you that. I haven't even talked with you. Where are you hearing these things?" I said, knowing full well where she heard them. I had long suspected that she heard the voices of demons and that they controlled her personality. I kept trying to point her toward the realization that she was listening to lies, but she refused to hear it. She was blinded to truth and *couldn't* see it. Her own personality was suffocated beneath thick bondage, and she was unable to entertain rational thoughts. She hung up on me in total disgust.

In all my life I never saw my mother forgive anything or anyone. She was an injustice-collector of the highest order. She had on the tip of her tongue the name of anyone who had ever wronged her and could tell you the complete incident in full detail. She could relive it with all the intensity of feeling as when it first happened. And so, just as she never forgave Dad for suggesting that she go to a mental hospital, she never forgave me for not coming to dinner at three in the morning.

Several months later, Michael and I took Christopher to visit my parents. When I walked into their house, I noticed the dining table was set and there was at least a quarter inch of dust on everything and cobwebs on the glasses.

"Why is the table so dirty?" I whispered to Dad. "The dishes are filthy."

"Your mother set that table some time around midnight the night before we called you at four thirty in the morning and you said you weren't coming. She got so angry she refused to put anything away. She wouldn't let *me* touch it either."

When I met Mother's cold stare, that familiar look of venom, it was clear that I was back on top of her hate list. She barely spoke to me, although she tried to be civil when Michael was in the room with us.

My husband, like many people, had thought of my mother as "such a nice woman" when he first met her. However, the first time we stayed with my parents for a couple days one Christmas early in our marriage, my mother couldn't keep up the front. She had to communicate with her voices, so she prowled all night speaking hateful things to those who were trying to kill her. She complained of people shooting her with laser guns and electronic rays and watching her through windows and mirrors and the TV. The FBI tortured her sexually, she said. I couldn't believe my ears. I'd never heard her say the word "sexually" in my entire life, and here she was being tortured sexually by the FBI! *Imagine how surprised they would be to hear that,* I thought to myself.

Even though Michael was initiated early on to my mother's insanity, he never saw her in a fit of rage. Only a select few people had ever witnessed that— one was my aunt who came to have her committed—and it was definitely something they would never forget. I had seen it repeatedly as a child, far more than anyone else. Michael was spared.

Mother's hatred of me persisted throughout the day we were there. I tried to ignore it, but it was impossible. When it came time for dinner, I said, "I'll set the table."

"The table's already set!" She spit out the words at me. "It's been set for four months, and you're going to eat off of it just the way it is."

"But it's dirty," I protested like a little girl trying to hide bitterness behind innocence. What was the matter with me that after all these years and all my healing and deliverance she was still able to reduce me to the basest of emotions? I was supposed to be a Christian adult and a leader in the church, yet I felt like slugging this mean old lady. It appeared that the only time I could have pity on this poor, emotionally-deformed person was when we were not in the same room. I was not able and would never be able to cope with her hatred of me in person. Michael and I cleared the table, washed all the dishes, and set the table again. Then we all sat down to a very solemn and tension-filled meal. We left the next morning after we realized we couldn't stay any longer, not even for Dad. In the car I said to my husband, "I can never go back there."

I wanted to obey God and honor my father and mother, but I was having a horribly difficult time with the mother part.

"You don't have to go there to be destroyed by her," Mary Anne had counseled me. "Honor her from afar. Don't feel guilty if you are released to stay away for a while. Give yourself time to be healed."

I tried to explain it to Dad, but he said, "Why don't you just walk out and ignore her the way I do?"

"I wish I could, Dad, but it just doesn't work that way for me. Here I am grown-up and with a family of my own, and yet I feel the same way around her as when I was a child."

He understood why I found her too upsetting to be around, and he agreed to come alone to *our* house for visits.

Now my prayers for my mother intensified.

"You're a Redeemer," I reminded God. "You redeem all things, Lord. I pray that You would redeem this relationship with my mother. I've never had a mother-daughter relationship. Make her whole so that this part of my life can be restored."

Then, as clearly as anytime in my life, I heard God speak to my heart. He said, "I am going to redeem that relationship, but I'm going to redeem it through your own daughter."

I blinked, swallowed hard, and said meekly to the all-knowing God of all creation, "But, Lord, I don't have a daughter."

The silence was deafening. As I waited for God's reply I thought, *I'll be close to forty if I have another child. My first pregnancy was horrendous. I don't think I can live through another one. I've always been defensive with anyone who suggested that we have another baby. God does not require of me beyond what I'm able.*

I continued to fight the idea for a long time, until I finally realized I was fighting the will of God. I knew He would love me whether I had another child or not, but if I wanted all the healing, wholeness, and blessings He had planned for me, I had to lay down my life again and surrender my will to His. Once Michael and I made the decision to obey God, I actually felt relief.

My relief turned to joy as I asked God not to let this pregnancy be like the first one, and He responded by comforting me with the words "I will see you through it." I thought that meant it would be better.

I was shocked, devastated, overwhelmed, and dismayed when this second pregnancy turned out to be physically even more severe than the first. Again, violent nausea took over my body, and I began losing weight. The pain was as if someone had poured boiling water through my veins. Unable to stand or sit up, I stayed flat on my back.

"God, why?" I cried. "Why this again? Have You deserted me?" But His words came back to me clearly: "I will see you through it." I realized He never said this time would be different; He never said that in this world we would have no problems. He said that in this world we will have trouble, but "I will see you through it."

My condition worsened, and I was admitted to the hospital and fed intravenously. My same doctor—one of the best obstetricians in the city—tried everything possible. He refused to give me medication for pain or nausea for fear that it might endanger the baby. I was grateful for his decision because I was sick enough that I might have taken anything for relief. Finally, my veins gave out, and as soon as they removed the IVs my condition worsened. I knew I needed a miracle, but I was too sick to pray anymore. All I could say was, "Help me, Jesus."

Every hour seemed like a week because of the pain and extreme nausea. I couldn't sit up. I couldn't read or watch television. I couldn't sleep. There was nothing I could do but lie in my hospital bed and cry. There was no relief.

Mary Anne visited often and read Scriptures to me hour upon hour. She massaged my legs, the only part of my body I could stand to have touched, and her eyes overflowed with compassion as she watched me getting worse.

One day I cried to her, "I was stupid to go ahead and get pregnant after what happened the last time. Why did I do this?"

She reminded me of the truth the pain had blinded me to. "You did it as a step of obedience to God, remember? There is great reward for obedience, you know."

"I'm sorry," I said, sobbing. "I just can't see it right now."

Then I heard God's voice again. "I will see you through it." I didn't know if this meant that I was going to die and be with the Lord or that the doctors were going to have to take the baby to spare my life. Those appeared to be the only two alternatives, and neither was my choice. I couldn't bear the thought of leaving my little boy, and I knew if I lost this child I would probably never be pregnant again.

That night I dreamed about holding a beautiful baby girl, with dark hair, sparkling chestnut-brown eyes, and long, dark eyelashes. The picture of her was so vivid and lifelike that it gave me happiness just to think of it. We still would not know the gender of the baby until birth.

When my doctor determined that there was nothing more he could do for me in the hospital, arrangements were made for me to go home. Pastor Jack called me that night before I was to be discharged from the hospital. He was disappointed that I had regressed to the point that they might have to take the baby.

I said, "I don't understand. I know God can heal me. I know I am supposed to have this baby, but the pain and nausea never let up, and I feel too weak to pray anymore."

There was love, compassion, and concern in my pastor's voice as he labored in prayer for me yet another time.

Sunday morning I was discharged from the hospital. The pain and nausea were worse than ever, and I was discouraged, to say the least. It was decided that if there was no change by the following Tuesday, taking the baby was the next step. There was nothing more that could be done, and time was running out.

At home in my own bed, little Christopher came into my room. He didn't run in happy to see me as he had always done before. He came in cautiously and kept his distance. I had not been a mother to him for four months, and now we were strangers. I couldn't hold him, read to him, or play games with him. Emotionally, he was leaving me behind. He politely said, "Hi, Mom," and then ran out of the room to continue his life. It broke my heart.

Bob and Sally, two very close friends, came to our house with their children to temporarily relieve Michael from the burden of this whole ordeal. They made the meals for the day and kept Michael and Christopher company. There was nothing they could do for me, so they left me alone and I was grateful.

Shortly after six that evening I almost jolted in bed. I sat up and said to myself, "What just happened?" It took a moment to realize that I suddenly felt no pain or nausea.

I sat on the edge of the bed for a few minutes to see if it would return. When nothing changed, I got up slowly and walked into the bathroom adjacent to our bedroom. I looked in the mirror at my thin face and hollow eyes, and then

I carefully walked back and sat on the bed for a moment. Still feeling no nausea or pain, I got up and walked into the den, where my husband was watching TV. He nearly fell off the couch as he sat up quickly and said, "What are you doing up?"

"I don't know," I said in disbelief. "I suddenly feel different. The pain is gone, and the nausea too. It may come back any minute," I added, revealing the extent of my great faith. After months of agony, I was afraid to hope that this feeling of physical relief could last.

Michael looked at me in amazement and said quietly, "Praise God!"

I walked slowly out of the den and down the long hall into the kitchen, where Sally was cleaning up the dinner dishes. I hadn't eaten much of anything for months, and even with intravenous feeding I felt very weak.

She turned and said in a startled voice, "What are *you* doing out here?"

"I don't know what happened, Sally. I suddenly feel better."

"Well, hallelujah!" she exclaimed, lifting up her voice. "Do you want something to eat just to prove that what you're saying is true?"

"Yes, quick, before it comes back again!"

She gave me a bowl of sliced pears and some plain dry toast. It tasted like a gourmet meal. I ate it all, thanking God for my reprieve. Even if it came back up, to be able to chew something and swallow was heaven.

We waited, but the nausea and pain didn't come back. Exhausted, I went to bed and slept through the night.

The next morning I still felt much better, but I decided to wait a day or two before I called Pastor Jack to tell him what happened in case it all came back. When I did call, I described to him in detail the events surrounding Sunday evening.

"Praise God, you've been healed!" he said right away.

"I have? Do you really think so?"

"Stormie," he said, sighing patiently, "I *know* so. That is the same time the congregation prayed for you in the Sunday evening service."

I was astonished. "You all prayed for me? You mean it won't come back?"

"No, you've been healed," he said with certainty.

He was right.

Just weeks away from my due date, I flew to New York to be with my husband at the Grammy Awards ceremony, where he won three Grammys for producing an album called *Christopher Cross*. Christopher was the first artist to win the four top awards—Album of the Year, Record of the Year, Song of the Year, and Best New Artist—all in one evening. It was an exciting time, and I thanked God that He made it possible for me to be a part of such a big night for my husband. I would never have been able to do that had not God done a miracle.

Soon after I returned home, the pretty little dark-haired girl with the chestnut-brown eyes and long, dark eyelashes I saw in my dream was born. We named her Amanda, meaning "worthy to be loved." Right away I could see that this time everything was different. I had no urges to be abusive. No times of losing control. No rage, no anger, no inkling of the former problem. I had been set free and healed of all that.

As soon as I was recovered enough from another Cesarean delivery, I concentrated on making up for lost time with Christopher. Every afternoon when Amanda was sleeping, I had a friend watch her while I took him someplace special—just the two of us. Although he was extremely proud of his little sister, it made him feel important and grown-up to kiss her goodbye and inform her that she was too little to go where we were going. In our three hours together, Christopher and I got acquainted again. We walked and we talked. We went to the park, to a children's movie, miniature golfing, to the toy store. This was *our* time, and within two weeks all that was damaged during those months of my infirmity was repaired.

From the moment Amanda was born, the healing began. Just like an open wound heals slowly day by day, I felt a wound in my emotions, in my heart somewhere, begin to heal. I went to my very first mother-daughter tea event at Amanda's school for Mother's Day. It was thrilling beyond description. I found myself feeling sorry for the two little children whose mothers didn't come. Always before that had been me. I never had a mother who came. Now I was getting to go as a mom.

Amanda's pretty brown eyes sparkled as she got up with her friends to sing the songs and recite the poem they had rehearsed for their mothers. Every few seconds she would steal a glance in my direction to see if I was watching her.

I was.

God had kept His promise to restore my lost mother-daughter relationship, and He did it over the following years through my own daughter. Who would have ever thought of that?

# 16

# Hidden Unforgiveness

From that time on, many different groups of people asked me to speak at their events. When my children were small, I accepted no more than one a month on a Saturday when my husband could stay home and take care of them. It was good for him to see how much time and effort it took. It was good for them to spend time with their dad. And it was good for me to get away for a day.

Whenever I spoke, I always included my story of how God restored me to wholeness. God specifically instructed me to include at least part of my testimony in every talk I gave, no matter what subject I was speaking on. He spoke to my heart, saying, "Tell the story of what I have done in your life. Don't worry about who has heard it and who has not. I am using for good what the enemy intended for evil." The two times I didn't include it, people came up to me afterward expressing their disappointment, saying something like, "I brought my friend here to hear your story and you didn't even mention it. I am so upset. I know it would have made a big difference in her life." I felt bad about that and resolved not to neglect to do that again.

Each time I told my story, without fail there was a surprising number of people who told me they were suffering from the same wounds and emotional scars I once had. They felt they were dying inside and needed to know there could be life before death for them. I was amazed at the response.

Another thing I often heard after I spoke was, "Do you ever get rid of the pain?" It was a frequent question from people who had been deeply hurt or abused as children. I knew immediately the pain they were referring to.

"I don't know," I replied. "I have received tremendous healing and freedom beyond anything I ever dreamed possible, but I don't know if you ever get *rid* of that pain."

The pain from a foundation of rejection is a constant "pain in the gut," and many people, like me, accept it as part of our life. It's with us everywhere we go. Before I met Jesus, I silenced my pain with methods that, in the long run, only served to make it worse. Even in my happiest moments, the pain was always there, waiting for the mere suggestion of rejection to bring it rushing in, reaffirming all of the negative feelings I had ever had about myself. After establishing my relationship with God through Jesus, I was able to take my pain to Him in prayer on a continual basis. It had certainly gotten much better and more controllable, but it was still there.

One day, Mary Anne called me into her office to tell me about a dream she'd had in which she believed God revealed to her why I still seemed to have such unrest in my soul. "You have unconfessed unforgiveness toward your father."

"What?" I exclaimed with indignation. "No way, Mary Anne. This time you're wrong."

"Honestly, Stormie, I would not have thought of that myself. I believe the dream I had was definitely from God."

I was silent.

"Pray about it. See what He says to you."

"You don't understand. My dad is a nice man and has never done anything bad to me. He never laid a hand on me except for one time at my mother's prodding. Why would I need to forgive him?"

"See what God says to you about it," she gently repeated.

On my way home I prayed, "God, what is Mary Anne talking about? Is there any truth to this?"

Then suddenly, like a flash of steel penetrating my heart, I nearly doubled over with pain. I saw myself in the closet again crying silently, *Why doesn't Dad ever open the door and let me out?* The thought of it was so painful that I started sobbing hysterically. Blinded by tears, I had to pull over on the freeway.

"God help me!" I struggled to get control over myself. In those moments, I clearly saw that I did indeed harbor unforgiveness toward my dad for never once coming to my rescue when I was a child. He never let me out of the closet. He didn't once save me from my mother's insanity. I had been let down by the one person who was my protector. The unforgiveness I harbored was unconfessed because I had never allowed myself to consciously think angry thoughts toward him.

I had learned just a couple of years prior to this that, when I confronted my dad about my childhood, much to my surprise, he didn't know about all the times Mother had locked me in the closet. Although it relieved my mind to hear that, it didn't heal the wound. And it didn't release me from the bondage of a lifetime of hidden unforgiveness toward him. I felt that if I were hanging over a cliff by my fingertips, any male authority in my life would walk on by and let me drop. I couldn't depend on anyone else to come through for me, so it took constant energy to keep myself together and I could never rest.

Mary Anne and her husband asked Michael and me to meet with them after a Good Friday service to pray for me to be free from all this hidden unforgiveness. Again, I agreed to fast for three days before that.

Oddly enough, along with all of this I started to feel that I was going crazy. I had heard there is a fine line between sanity and insanity, and I suddenly felt as though I were walking on it. After a few years of *not* feeling that way, I couldn't understand why all of a sudden there was a definite sensation of losing my mind—far stronger than anything I had ever experienced before. I'd often been concerned about ending up like my mother, but I had never felt even close to that until now.

Good Friday arrived, and we all met as planned in the counseling office. I

WONDERWORD

HOW TO PLAY: All the words listed below appear in the puzzle — horizontally, vertically, diagonally and even backward. Find them, circle each letter of the word and strike it off the list. The leftover letters spell the

...y unforgiveness for my dad, and as I did, the ray of steel penetrated ...gain, only this time it unleashed a torrent of emotion unlike any I'd ...ed in my adult life. I recognized it as the pain I had felt as a small child ...a closet with no one to help me. It was the same pain that would periodically ...well up in me with such force that I had to withdraw from my friends ...ol, or double over against a bathroom stall at CBS.

...e pain came to the surface in full force. I sobbed grieving sobs from deep ...y being. They were sobs I had held back rigidly in my throat for years ...cause my mother threatened to beat me if I cried. The pain felt to me as if I ...was giving birth to something bigger than my body could deliver—something tangible, something immeasurable.

Mary Anne and her husband anointed me with oil, laid their hands on my head, and commanded in the name of Jesus that any oppressive spirit that had a hold on my life be broken. One final surge of pain wracked my body, and then it was over. A new inner peace settled over me.

With the expulsion of that deeply buried unforgiveness and rage, the devil's final stronghold in my life was destroyed. I could see clearly now that the repressed unforgiveness had led to a type of mental imbalance. Could that be what had happened to my mother? That all of her unforgiveness internalized to the point that her view of life became warped by it? I was sure it wasn't the only thing that led to mental imbalance, but I knew for certain that a sound mind cannot coexist with deep unforgiveness and rage. There is a direct tie between forgiveness and wholeness.

I also saw that deliverance is a process that happens in different ways at different times. Sometimes it happens simply by spending time in God's presence and walking in obedience to Him, such as the way I was delivered from my fear of knives. Sometimes it happens by crying out to God in prayer and exalting Him in praise, the way I did when I discovered my potential for child abuse. Sometimes it happens in the counseling office with the guidance of trained and qualified Christian counselors, as it did when I was set free of paralyzing depressions. But no matter how it happens, it's only Jesus—the Deliverer—who can truly set us free. He is the One True Light who comes to burn away the darkness that tries to separate us from all God has for us.

The next morning I noticed distinctly that I didn't feel at all as if I were going crazy. I felt completely normal, and the sensation of pending insanity never came back. I believe I was set free from a spirit of insanity. I was not possessed by it because I had Jesus, and the Spirit of Christ living in me, and He crowds out all else. But the enemy knows our weaknesses, and he comes to oppress us with reminders of them. My longtime fear of becoming like my mother was the perfect condition to oppress me with those thoughts.

I saw that the realm of darkness never stops attacking us. Our job is to get free of everything we cling to that is not of God. *Our responsibility is to know God more every day*, I realized.

*That's because everything we don't know about God will be used against us by the enemy of our soul.*

For the first time in my life, I saw how little I knew about my own father. No one ever volunteered information about him, and I never thought to ask. I had always subconsciously viewed him as a one-dimensional stick figure, but now that I was set free from all my unforgiveness, I discovered aspects of his personality and qualities of his character I had never acknowledged. He was the oldest of eight children—three boys and five girls—and because of this he carried a great deal of responsibility in the home. He was raised on a farm in Pennsylvania by devout Christian parents, although his dad was extremely strict and not affectionate. His father was the superintendent at the church and his mother was the organist. I was surprised by this because I had never heard Dad say the words "church" or "God" in my whole life.

"Why didn't you ever go to church once you left home, Dad?" I questioned after he surprised me with this new information.

"In order to get to church we had to walk a mile-and-a-half through the fields," he answered. "We went two times on Sunday and every Thursday night no matter if there was hail, rain, or snow. When we got there we sat nearly four hours at a time on uncomfortable wooden benches while the preacher ranted and raved about hellfire and brimstone. It was boring as could be, and children weren't allowed to move or make a sound. I've always believed in God, but I decided that once I left home, I was *never* going to go through that kind of torture again."

I heard from other relatives that Dad was a very handsome man and that many women were after him. But he was shy and paid no attention to any of them until he met my mother when he was in his early thirties. She was 24, and he was dazzled by her beauty and charming party personality. He fell in love with her and always remained in love with his first impression of her, even after no trace of it remained in reality. Apparently, the hope of her "someday snapping out of it" and returning to normal kept him going.

After I forgave Dad, I could see how much he really did love *me*. He never showed it openly because he wasn't comfortable doing that, but his love was there just the same. I discovered that even though a parent may love a child deeply, unless the child *perceives* that love he won't *feel* loved. Realizing this made me become more deliberately affectionate with my own children.

Six months after that Good Friday counseling session, I had come to a new level of peace and rest like I had never before imagined. I spoke before a large group of people and told my story of God's total restoration. When I finished, there was a question-and-answer time in which a lady stood up and asked, "Do you ever get rid of the pain?"

With joy I smiled and answered, "Yes! For the first time in my life I can say that you really do get rid of the pain. It doesn't happen overnight, but it does happen."

# 17

# Peace Beyond Understanding

My mother had not left the house in five years, so spending another Christmas without her was not unusual. Dad came to our home, along with my sister and her family, and we all celebrated together. Part of the gift that Michael and I gave Dad that year was a trip east to visit his relatives. We presented it to him early so he could leave and be back in time for Christmas Day at our house. The day after Christmas, he planned to return home to his farm.

During this time no one worried about my mother because she always loved being alone. It was her opportunity to talk to the voices in her head and carry on unrestricted. A giant freezer in the garage was stocked full of food, so she was not wanting for anything to eat.

When Dad returned home after Christmas he found that she had not done any dishes for the two weeks he was gone and had not eaten much of anything during the last few days. Our first thought was that her characteristic refusal to do housework had caused her to stop eating when she ran out of dishes. When it appeared that she wanted to eat but couldn't, Dad concluded she must have the flu. Her mental condition had gone down at an accelerated rate during the past two years, so communicating with her was difficult. It was impossible to get an answer from her that made any sense. As she progressively lost touch with reality, she barely seemed like a human being anymore.

Just a few months earlier, Mother and Dad's little dog became sick and died. Mother refused to believe the dog was dead. She placed the body in the middle of her own bed and every day put food in its mouth, poured water down its throat, and talked to the dead body as if it were a living dog. Whenever Dad came near the dog or mentioned burying it, Mother grew hysterical. This finally convinced Dad that it was time to see about having her committed. He went for help but found that new laws made commitment much more difficult. He had to prove that she might physically harm herself or someone else. Because he could not prove that, his hands were tied.

After the dog had been dead on her bed for over a week, the smell was pungent enough to keep Dad awake at night in his bedroom down the hall. He knew he had to take action. Because my mother slept all day and prowled the house talking to voices all night, Dad waited until she was sound asleep. About midmorning he crept in, took the little corpse off the bed, and buried it in the field in back of the house. Anticipating what would happen when she awoke, he dug the hole very deep and covered it well.

When Mother woke up and found the dog missing, she was angry and hysterical.

"Where's the dog?'" she demanded of my father.

"I've buried her. She's dead," he said with finality.

"She's not dead. You've buried her alive!" she screamed repeatedly as she ran for the shovel. She dug everywhere searching for the dog. She even dug right in the place where Dad had buried her, but the grave was deep enough that Mother never found her. She finally gave up looking.

After that, Mother's complaints about people shooting her increased. "They're shooting me with laser beams in my stomach and my breast. They're beaming rays into my brain. They want information, but I won't give it to them," she said to me when I called.

I pitied her, but not enough to visit. I no longer hated her, but her verbal attacks on me were unceasing. She acted as if she despised me, and even though I understood that it was self-hatred turned outward, I couldn't bear to be with her.

My sister always got along decently with my mother and visited her periodically. After Christmas she reported that Mother looked very bad; she had lost a lot of weight, her face was puffy, and her skin was yellow. My dad remained firm in his belief that she had the flu.

Just before Michael and I were to take the children on a family vacation to Hawaii, I called Dad to ask about Mother.

"She's better," he said. "She's staying in bed and I'm bringing meals to her. She's eating well now—not throwing up."

"Do you want me to come and help you with her?"

"No, no. She's doing fine now," he assured me.

On the morning after our arrival in Hawaii, I got up before everyone else and went for a walk on the beach. This was my alone time to talk to God. It seemed I could always hear Him more clearly away from telephones, obligations, deadlines, and people, and close to the beauty of His creation. When I returned to our room at the hotel, everyone was just getting up. We dressed and went out to eat. When we returned to our room after breakfast, I saw the red light blinking on the telephone signaling that someone had called and left a message. Immediately I sensed it was something serious. I called the front desk and received a message to contact my sister at my parents' home. I quickly dialed, anticipating bad news, for neither my sister or Dad had ever called me on vacation before.

My dad answered. "Your mother's very ill, Stormie," he said with a distressed voice. "We're trying to get her to a doctor, but she won't go. There's an ambulance here now, but she's locked herself in the bathroom and won't come out for anybody."

"Where's Suzy?"

"She's talking to her through the bathroom door."

*How sick can she be*, I wondered, *if she's strong enough to lock herself in the bathroom?*

I heard Dad yell, "Suzy, Stormie's on the phone!"

Suzy's voice betrayed the seriousness of the situation as she spoke. "Mom's really sick. You wouldn't recognize her. She must have lost sixty pounds. She's skin and bones and she looks awful. I think she's dying." Her voice sounded suddenly mature.

"Are you sure?" I asked in disbelief. I thought, *How can it be that just a few days ago Dad said she was getting better and now she is dying?*

"She refuses to come out of the bathroom and go with the ambulance attendants who are here waiting. What should I do? She's in pain. She needs help." Her voice broke.

"Suzy, she's probably afraid of the men. Maybe she thinks they're going to kill her. If you can't get her to go with them, then let them go. After they're gone and she comes out of the bathroom, ask her if she will let you take her to the hospital. You are the only one she will listen to. Tell her you can't stand to see her in pain and they will give her something to help her. Tell her you won't leave her, that you'll stay with her."

"Okay," she said with conviction and direction in her voice.

"We'll take the first flight out. I'll call and tell you what time we're coming in," I said and hung up the phone.

There was a sudden urgency inside of me. I had to get home. "God, please help me to get there before she dies," I prayed as I dialed the airline.

There were no flights with seating for four people until midnight, and I wasn't going without my family. I was afraid to see Mother alone without Michael and my children.

It took us the rest of the day to pack, return the rental car, check out of the hotel, and make call after call to see if we could take an earlier flight.

Before leaving for the airport, I spoke again with Suzy. She'd followed my suggestion and Mother had agreed to go to the hospital. Suzy and Dad carried her to the car and then drove her to the hospital's emergency entrance. Suzy stayed with her until she was admitted, given something for pain, and fell asleep.

"What did the doctor say?" I asked.

"Cancer. She's not going to make it. They're just going to keep giving her something for pain."

"Oh, no!" I said, filled with guilt over not being there, as well as sadness over my mother's intense suffering.

"Stormie," Suzy said after a brief pause, "don't feel guilty if you don't make it before she dies. She's so bad that you don't want to see her like this."

There was silence as I choked back tears and tried to swallow and speak. "Thanks, Suzy. I can't tell you how much I appreciate your saying that." As much as I wanted to see my mother before she died, I also feared lifelong anger from my sister and dad for not being there.

We boarded the plane around midnight and arrived in Los Angeles at eight in the morning. We went home, dumped the contents of the suitcases on the floor and repacked them with warm clothing while Michael fixed us all something quick to eat and made beds in the back of the car for the children to sleep.

I called my parents' home and there was no answer. I then called the hospital and demanded that they put me through to my mother's room.

"She's in critical condition," the receptionist protested.

"I'm her daughter!" I insisted.

Suzy's husband, Louis, answered the phone.

"Louie, we're leaving right now from our house. How is she doing?"

"I don't know if you'll make it," he said, his voice noticeably shaken.

"You can't be serious. You mean she won't last four more hours?" I asked in horror. I couldn't believe it. This was all happening so fast.

"You don't know what she's like." His voice quivered. "She doesn't look like your mother anymore, Stormie. She's not the same person."

"We'll be there as fast as we can, Lou. We're coming straight to the hospital." He gave me directions, and I could hear my dad and sister talking as Mother moaned in the background.

We piled in the car and nearly flew there, hitting every green light and no traffic. In the car I broke down and began to sob. "Please, God, let me get there before she dies. Please, God, don't let her die before I see her."

I looked in the backseat and met two pairs of very concerned little brown eyes staring back at me.

"I'm okay," I reassured Christopher and Amanda. "Mommy's just afraid that Grandma will die before we get there."

"That will be sad," said seven-year-old Christopher.

"I'll be sad too," said almost three-year-old Amanda, not fully understanding, but wanting to be like her big brother.

I had always been honest with my children and had shared with them truthfully as much as I thought they could understand. Christopher knew that my mother had mistreated me as a child, but he understood that it was because she was sick. "Grandma has always loved *you*," I reassured the two of them.

I prayed silently all the way there. Something inside of me hoped that Mother and I would see each other and that things would be different. Maybe she would be in her right mind and could let go of her hatred of me for a few minutes and we could communicate as a mother and daughter. I even had wild dreams of us telling each other we were sorry for the ways we hurt each other, and maybe we could even say, "I love you."

On the way there, I thought back to all the times Mother complained about people shooting her in the breast, the head, and the stomach. It never occurred to any of us that she was talking about real pain.

I thought about my periodic calls to talk to Dad, and how he always gave the phone to Mother. She consistently answered in the same unfriendly tone.

"Hi, Mom. How are you doing?" I would chirp in my most phony happy voice.

"How do you think I'm doing?" she would angrily begin, and then proceed to vomit all the garbage that surrounded her days. From then on I couldn't get a word in, so I would lay the phone down on the bed and check in about every five minutes. She would still be talking, not fazed in the least that I had contributed nothing to the conversation. Thirty or forty minutes later I would pick up the phone and say very loudly, "I have to go now, Mother. Goodbye." My dad mentioned that after talking with me my mother always felt a little better and didn't have to complain as much to him. I looked upon those telephone times with my mother as saving my dad's life.

I thought about the last time I visited my mother and dad. Out of the blue, she had popped into the den where I was sitting alone and said, "All those times I locked you in a closet...that never bothered you, did it?" The pitch of her voice came down at the end, implying that of course it never bothered me as opposed to asking a true question and looking for an honest answer.

I was so shocked I could hardly speak. Was this the same woman who never admitted doing anything wrong in her life? Granted, she made it clear she knew this closet thing was no big deal and that she was just curious, but she *did* at least admit to doing it.

I pitied her enough to not tell her the truth, but I still had sufficient fleshly qualities in me to caustically remark, "Oh, no, Mother. I loved every minute of it."

My snideness went totally unobserved. Mother heard what she wanted to hear, and with a slight smile she replied, "I didn't think it bothered you." Then she returned to what she was doing in the kitchen. Part of me rejoiced because my mother had finally admitted she'd locked me in the closet. What provoked her to mention it after all these years I really couldn't imagine. Maybe unconfessed sin never lets a person rest no matter what the circumstances are.

The drive was two-and-a-half-hours long, far short of the four hours it usually took us. Michael dropped me off in front of the hospital, and I quickly ran up the long walkway to the main lobby while he parked the car. I asked for my mother's room number, and when the receptionist couldn't locate it my heart pounded. I feared that it was too late and she had been taken out of her room.

"No, here it is. She is in Room three A, right down the hall."

The hospital was very small, and it took only seconds to run to her room and open the door. There was no one in the double-occupancy room but two old, very sick-looking ladies, neither of whom I recognized as my mother. The one farthest away was unconscious and hooked up to many wires, tubes, and a respirator. She had no teeth. My mother had teeth. She had never allowed a dentist to lay a hand on her.

The other woman was extremely thin and frail, her pale blue eyes staring off to the side in a pained and hopeless expression. *I must have the wrong room,* I thought, and started to leave. But as I took a second look just to make sure, I saw that the pale blue eyes belonged to my mother. I hardly recognized her tiny frame.

"Mom," I said softly. "Mom, it's me, Stormie."

There was no response.

I positioned myself so that her blue eyes stared directly at me. They were unseeing.

"Mom!" I began to cry. "Mom, you're gone, aren't you? I'm too late."

I felt her. She was still warm. She must have died only a few seconds before I arrived.

I took her hand and held it in mine and began to cry. I laid my head on her chest and sobbed into the blanket. I didn't cry because I missed my mother or our relationship. There had never been a relationship. I cried for all the things that never were. For all that never was to be between us. For the joy of life she never knew. I cried for the pain of a small girl who stamped her foot and talked back to her pregnant mother and then never saw her again because her mother went to the hospital that night and died. I cried for a young teenager who felt she was responsible for every death in her family. I cried for a woman who lived in fear, unforgiveness, bitterness, and rage at God and never knew His love and healing and deliverance. I cried for a woman who couldn't accept her daughter's forgiveness because she was unable to forgive herself. I cried for a person who never became what God created her to be. I grieved for all that, and knew it must be what God feels about *us* when we strain and strive and get ourselves into horribly painful situations when all we need to do is turn to Him and surrender.

I looked up at her face again and stroked her hair. I cried for all the years of my life I wasn't able to touch her with any affection. She would never allow it.

Oddly enough, even though I very much wanted to see my mother alone one last time, as I had prayed on the way there, I felt God's presence and peace. If He had wanted me to see her alive, He could have gotten me there minutes earlier. But perhaps she would have gathered what strength she had left and screamed some horrible and cruel words at me and I would have been left with that final memory for the rest of my life. I trusted that God knew best.

With still no other conscious person in the room, I did something that might have seemed disrespectful and odd. I lifted the covers to look at Mother's body.

Her legs were beautiful—thin, with milky white skin, yet exquisitely formed. Her stomach was distended. I lifted her gown and put my hand on the area where I thought her liver would be located, and I felt a large, hard mass. I then touched her left breast and I felt an enormous lump the size of half a grapefruit. It was just as I had suspected from Suzy's telephone description: breast cancer spread to the liver and the brain. I marveled at how Mother must have suffered all those years without ever allowing anyone to help her. What a horrifying, awful death. It sickened me to think of the agonizing pain she must have experienced.

I pulled her gown down, laid the covers neatly back over her, and picked up her hand again. The fingers were getting cold now. I stared at her face. Her blue eyes were extra big because of her extreme weight loss. I had always thought of her as large and hideous. Now she looked tiny, frail, and pretty.

As her body cooled and became stiff, the finality of it hit me. Suddenly my mind flashed to the little church we had attended when I was 14. I remembered how she talked about God and Jesus as if they were real to her, and how dedicated she was for those few months until she threw out the large family Bible in a fit of rage. She never spoke about God again except to say that He knew people were trying to kill her but wasn't able to help. Now I felt peace about her, as if God was saying, "It's okay, Stormie. Your mother is with Me. She doesn't hurt anymore. She's not crazy anymore. I've got her."

Actually, it was a strangely peaceful time, unlike what I would have expected. Death didn't feel so bad. Of course, that was easy for me to say. I wasn't the one who had died. But it seemed natural—like a normal part of life.

Finally, two nurses walked in, and when they realized that my mother was dead they asked me to leave the room. As I did, my husband was just coming down the hall with the children. "She's dead, Michael," I whispered.

When he and I were allowed back in Mother's room, I saw that the nurses had closed her eyes, folded her arms, and straightened the sheet across her body. As we stood there silently, the doctor entered. He was a kindly man in his sixties.

"I'm very sorry about your mother," he said. "There was nothing we could do. She had cancer in her breast and liver, and possibly a brain tumor as well. Her liver was five times the normal size."

He expressed shock at how advanced the cancer had become before she permitted anyone to give her medical aid.

"Doctor, I'm grateful for all that you've done for my dad through these last five years, and I'm thankful you were able to alleviate Mother's pain in the last few hours of her life," I assured him.

"The cancer was so bad that even if your dad had brought her to me a year ago, I don't believe I could have saved her." He had known about Mother's mental condition because my dad had confided in him and sought his advice, though no one knew she was *physically* ill as well. "The medical expenses would have been tremendous for your dad, and it wouldn't have made any difference anyway. That cancer had been growing in her for many years. It was really better this way."

"I believe so too. What happens now?"

"We need to call your dad," Michael said, and he left to find a phone. Dad was unprepared for Mother's death. He had no idea she was that sick, and the shock of it put him to bed. Michael and I handled all the arrangements.

I picked out the most beautiful casket I could find and ordered large, colorful bouquets of flowers because I knew she would have thought them beautiful. I chose a burial plot under a big shade tree because she always loved trees. I also bought her new pretty underwear, and as I handed my money to the cashier, tears I had been choking back suddenly flooded down my cheeks and I began to sob. I was struck by the remembrance of all the times I had wanted to buy things for my mother, like I was buying now, but she would never receive them from me. Now I was doing it for her funeral. The cashier gave me my change, handed me my purchase, and looked at me with concern. She didn't say anything, though, and I was glad.

My sister took our mother's death hard. I had trouble understanding why, because I never realized that they had a relationship. I made the mistake of assuming that Suzy was the same as I was—wanting the same things, experiencing the same things. But the opposite was true; there was nothing similar about us. Suzy talked back to my mother; I cowered in a corner. She got angry and showed it; I got hurt and kept my rage inside. She had a relationship with my mother, even though she was not a good mother. I had none. Suzy felt grief; I felt relief. Even as children, we had been raised in two completely different worlds. My mother relentlessly abused me; by contrast she neglected Suzy. It is almost as if my mother thought that she had really overdisciplined me and so she would not discipline Suzy at all. But Mother never thought rationally about anything. I didn't realize any of that until now.

I was happy that I had no hard feelings toward my mother—no unforgiveness, no anger, no resentment, no unsettled scores. God had cleansed it all. Everything had been accomplished before her death, and I would never have to deal with those things again.

Word of Mother's death traveled quickly among family and friends. We received many phone calls, and I was shocked when one woman mentioned how much my mother had cared about me.

"Your mother was always very proud of you," said Anita, a longtime family friend who remained loyal to us even though Mother had often treated her rudely.

"Mother was proud of me?" I asked astonished, not believing what I'd heard.

"When you starred in your high school play, she was very pleased. And she was proud of all your television shows. She never attended any of them because she thought the people who were trying to kill her might want to kill you too."

"I can't believe what you're saying, Anita. Why didn't she ever give me even the slightest indication that she felt that way?"

"You know your mother, Stormie. She had very strange ideas. She believed that if she were ever to tell you *anything* good about yourself, you would be spoiled. I'm sorry you never knew your mother when she was younger. She was a lovely woman, she really was. The mental disease took over her life and disguised anything recognizable of her good qualities."

Unsuccessfully choking back tears, I said, "Thank you, Anita. That means a lot."

After my mother's funeral, we stayed a number of days to help Dad and then drove up every weekend for several months. His house was dirty, dark, and depressing because Mother never allowed anyone in to clean or paint. Her room was filled with thick cobwebs that hung down just like in an old horror movie. The bed was backed up to the closet so that the headboard covered the doors, preventing them from being opened. Inside, the closet was filled to the ceiling with old, dirty clothes and every canceled check, receipt, letter, and magazine clipping she had ever possessed.

Dad asked me to sort through her things. I didn't blame him. He'd been through too much to do it himself. The sorting was far beyond what I anticipated. I found in the house and the adjacent shed nearly every dress, coat, shoe, or purse that I, my sister, and my mother had ever owned. It was like reliving my past to see it all. I knew she never threw anything away, but I had never imagined the extent of her hoarding. It was another sign of her mental sickness and fear.

Michael and I decided that it was crucial to my dad's health that the house have a face-lift, and the job was too monumental for any of us. So we hired people to paint inside and out and to install new carpets, drapes, and bedspreads. With each step I could feel my dad's spirit lift. The unhappy memories faded and the place felt new. So did Dad.

Amid the cleaning I found the old green diary I wrote in when I was 14. I had thrown it out, but Mother had obviously found it in the trash and retrieved it. Over the next few days I read it from cover to cover. My life back then was far worse than I even remembered. I was shocked at my ignorance; I knew nothing of the right way to live. As I finished reading the diary, I thanked God for the reminder of how far He had brought me. Time and much healing had dimmed all that pain in my memory.

I gazed out the window to the yard, where Dad was pushing little Amanda in the swing he had constructed for her and her brother in the large willow tree. She giggled and chirped, "Higher, Gampa, higher!"

Over the past few weeks of cleaning and sorting, it was Dad who had basically taken care of Chris and Amanda. They went with him to feed the cows, pick the oranges, and ride the little horse he had. Their mutual love was apparent. Now that Mother was gone, we were at liberty to visit Dad anytime, and he was free to be himself. As he blossomed, so did our relationship. He had always been a social individual, but a shadow of fear that he would say something wrong in front of my mother and set her off had shrouded his every word. Now all of that was gone.

For years he had been hard of hearing. After Mother's death I suddenly noticed one day that his hearing was normal. Could it be that in order to cope with her he had stopped listening? Was that an act of survival? Maybe that's why he didn't suspect she was dying. She had complained for so long that he had partially tuned her out. I used to be impatient with Dad's hesitant speech and poor hearing. Could it be that all these years I blamed him for things that were just a part of his coping with my mother?

I saw what a great man my father really was. Even though Mother had been heartlessly cruel to him, he still took good care of her until she died. Most other men would have left years ago. Once he developed a painful case of shingles and was so sick he couldn't get out of bed. Mother made a huge dinner and refused to give him anything at all to eat. In spite of that, he brought her every meal in bed during the weeks before she died, and he harbored no ill feeling toward her. He never even said a critical word about her after she died. His example of forgiveness was greater than any other I had ever seen.

"You can't hold a grudge. You gotta forgive and forget," he said over and over. Mother's death brought no regret to him. He had given above and beyond the call of duty.

# 18

# Confronting the Past

A s I sorted through my mother's things, I found in an old chest a drawer full of photos, papers, and things that had value to her. I discovered my old baby book that someone had given her as a gift. With my dad's permission I brought it home. It took me a while to gather the courage to look through it because I was almost afraid of what I would find in it. It wasn't as bad as I thought. In fact, I found my mother's own handwriting, under the first words I had said as a small child, one of the entries was, "What Stormie says when she is put in the closet." And one of the things I said was, "It's dark in here. I can't see anything." That was, in some strange way, very healing to me. It was as though, in her own sick way, she thought that was normal. And she admitted what she had done as a regular practice.

During that early morning walk along the beach in Hawaii where I talked to the Lord, He had spoken to my heart that it was okay to start writing the book about my life and how He saved, delivered, restored, and transformed me—how God has freedom for each of us from even the darkest and most hopeless circumstances of our lives. I had been working on the book for some time in my journals, but I didn't want to release a book about my mother while she was still alive. I always held out hope that she would be healed and come to know all God had for her. Telling the truth about her might keep her from ever coming to know Him. I couldn't do anything to hinder that. But I felt released by God that morning to tell the story, even though she was still alive. Obviously, He knew she would only be alive one more day.

Writing was my most treasured thing to do because I found it liberating. Through writing I could express my deepest, most pent-up thoughts, ideas, hopes, and dreams. I felt that writing this book would bring closure to me as well.

That summer I attended the Christian Bookseller's Convention, and a very kind young man named Bill approached me as I was walking past the Harvest House Publishers booth on my way to the publisher of my health book and exercise video I had releasing that season. He knew who I was and asked if by chance I had another book on my heart that I wanted to write because his company wanted to consider it for publication.

"Yes, as a matter of fact, I do have a book I am writing. I haven't shown it to anyone yet," I replied. I told him what it was about and he gave me his card and asked me to please let him and his company see some of it as soon as it was ready. I told him I would.

When I sent Bill what I had already finished in the book, Harvest House Publishers flew me to Oregon, where their company was located. I met Bob Hawkins Sr., the founder and president of the company, along with his staff. Bill was there as well. I also met Bob Hawkins Jr., who was fresh out of college and working at the company. They were all wonderfully kind and felt like family to me. They offered me a contract.

After I signed the contract, I began to *officially* write the book, and that is when all hell broke loose in my life. It was my first major experience with starting a project for God's kingdom of light and experiencing the realm of darkness attacking me in every way possible.

In order to write that book, I had to go back and relive everything that happened in great detail. I had to experience everything all over again. It was sheer hell having to relive all that, in the detail I needed to, in order to write it accurately. I had to face every bad memory all over again. I had to confront every miserable incident with all of its repulsiveness. There was not a day of writing that I did not end up crying with gut-wrenching sobs from the deepest part of my being.

I knew I couldn't effectively write about my past unless I faced it head-on. I had to bring it all before God and forgive myself, my mother, my father, and the people who suspected something was going on but never attempted to rescue me in any way. I had to relive feelings of abandonment, sadness, hopelessness, futility, anxiety, fear, and outrage, which all came back in full force. The resentment and bitterness I had because I started so far behind everyone else and had to work twice as hard to try and catch up. Even anger at God for allowing it to go on so long, although no one prayed for it to be any different—at least to my knowledge. It was awful. More than I could handle on most days.

One day I was writing about the rejection of the children on the playground that I mentioned earlier in this book. I sobbed and sobbed because to relive those deep hurts revealed how my heart had broken so deeply with no affection to heal it, and I lost hope at that point. I never felt hope again until I came to know the Lord. I felt so devastated that day when I was writing about it that I called Diana to ask her to pray with me about it.

Diana and Andrew had moved to another town about an hour away from us, and they had a baby boy. We were still praying several times a week by phone until a lump had been found in her breast during a routine checkup and then we prayed nearly every day. They did a lumpectomy and she was to hear soon what the results were.

"It's breast cancer," she said when she heard my voice. We both cried. I never mentioned my problems again to her. We prayed almost daily over the next months as she went on to have her breast removed and reconstructed, with chemotherapy and radiation in between. Less than a year after that it all repeated when cancer was found in her other breast. But this time after a year of treatment she lost her battle and went to be with the Lord. I was heartbroken. And I needed to take care of her eight-year-old son until his father could care for him. I missed Diana terribly, and seeing her son every day both helped and hurt. He reminded me so much of her that I keenly felt the loss—both his and his father's—as well as my own. They eventually moved to another state where living was cheaper and easier.

After I finished writing the book, I had to get my dad to read it and sign a paper saying it was okay to publish it. There were many intimate details about his life that would be revealed in it, and he had to sign off on it.

Michael and I drove up to his farm for dinner, and he started reading the book after we went to bed that night. I was terribly nervous about what he would think when he found out all of the bad things I had done. When I got up early the next morning, he was still sitting in the same recliner, with the book open on his lap, and he was looking out the window. He said he had been up all night and had just finished reading it. My heart pounded as I asked, "What did you think of the book?"

He paused for a second and said, "Well, you made your mother look good."

Tears came to my eyes. I felt such relief. It was true that I didn't tell how bad my mother really was, because I didn't think people could handle reading about it. She did some disgusting things, and although I had to face those things again, I could not include them. The fact that he acknowledged how bad she really was made me forever grateful that he understood. And he never once mentioned all the terrible things I had done.

After the book came out, the response was overwhelming. At the time I was writing the book I had no idea of the magnitude of what the testimony of coming out of darkness into the light actually meant for other people. It was far more than I ever anticipated. I received stacks and boxes full of letters from people all over the United States who went through similar experiences. They had not read any book that talked about it from the perspective of God's restoration and all He has for each of us as we step into His liberating presence. I had no idea the extent of emotional damage and scars that countless people kept hidden within them every day. The most amazing thing to me was that we were not alone. Many others were going through the same things, and relating to one another was extremely helpful.

I tried to respond to every letter and did so for a number of years, but then it became impossible. All I could do was read the letters and emails and pray for them. That is, until one particular person made it difficult for me to respond from that time forward.

# 19

# The Follower

The young woman was waiting for me when I picked up my children from school. Her son was in the same class as my son, although I had never met him. She was kind and sweet. She respectfully told me her name was Sandy* and that she had read my autobiography, *Stormie*, and related to my being abused as a child. She, too, had experienced something very similar with one of her parents, although I gathered it was not her mother who, she informed me, had paid for her grandson to go to this little Christian grade school. Plus, I gathered her abuse was of a sexual nature, which I had always thought of as male initiated and far more damaging to the soul of a child than any other form of abuse. She thanked me for giving her hope that she could one day recover from her past.

She asked where we attended church, and I told her.

Every day after school when I went to pick up my children, she waited to talk to me. We had pleasant conversations about recovering from emotional trauma. I met her son, her husband, and her mother, who all seemed to be a nice family.

On Sunday morning we went to church, and I dropped off my children in their respective classrooms as usual, but as I entered the church sanctuary, Sandy was there waiting for me at the door. I was happy to see they had decided to attend church there. As it turned out, they lived in an apartment close by.

Her husband had a business that helped homeowners with the maintenance of their home, so when she told me that their business was extremely slow, I hired them to do some work on my father's house. We had helped him move into a home about an hour away from us. When I saw the quality of their work, I asked them to do some maintenance on our house as well.

Sandy mentioned she needed to have her hair repaired because she had tried to dye her very dark hair a light shade of blond and totally fried it. She asked who and where my hair dresser was, and I told her. She also found out what stores I went to and what services I went to at church. All the while I believed I was helping her, I did not realize I was walking into a trap.

Gradually, nearly every place I went, Sandy would be out front waiting for me. I realized how terribly needy she was, and she felt I had all the answers to help her rise above her emotional torment. I tried to point her to the Lord in every way, but she insisted that she knew I was the only one who could help her. I told her that no one can do that but the Lord and a good counselor. I learned from her husband that he was painfully aware of her problem, but he also hoped I could help her.

When I realized what was happening over the next couple months, I tried to steer her toward professional help, but she was fixated on me fixing everything *for* her. She said she thought I could become the mother she never had.

The more I tried to loosen myself from her tentacles that were frighteningly everywhere by that time, the more she tried to take over my life. Soon she began acting bizarrely and calling my home 30 to 40 times a day with demonic-sounding voices threatening to kill my children if I didn't help her. It became apparent, and was confirmed by her husband, that she had multiple personalities. We didn't know what each one was capable of, because now she was coming to our home in the middle of the night and climbing over our fence into the backyard and looking in our windows. She stated on our answering machine exactly what she saw in the yard, and that confirmed she was indeed there. Michael and I prayed and prayed for God to remove this terrifying burden from us.

We called the police, and they said to get a lawyer. My husband and I went to a Christian lawyer friend for help, and he advised us to take her to court to seek a restraining order against her. Even though she appeared in court and the judge sternly warned her to stop stalking me and my family, it didn't slow her down. The phone calls and threats kept coming. Afraid for our lives, we called the police a number of times, but we were always told that they couldn't do anything unless the person had broken into the house and threatened our lives from the inside.

"It's too late by then," I said, trying to reason with a policeman who came to our house. "Something has to be done *before* that!"

"I'm sorry, but the law restricts us," he said. "We can't do anything until the stalker has broken in."

"That's terrible! What am I supposed to do? What do other people do in this situation? What would you advise that we do?"

"You could hire bodyguards or move somewhere else."

"Where do you get bodyguards? Do you know of a company that provides them?"

He gave me the name of a reputable security company providing that service, and we called them immediately. We hired two bodyguards to protect our lives for ten hours at night so we could sleep. And they were expensive. For the ten-hour shift each man was paid $125. We needed to have two men and one car at our house every night by 8:00 p.m., and they would watch through the night until 6:00 in the morning. That was $250 per night. Every night. It was outrageously expensive and completely unsustainable, but we felt we had no other choice at that moment. The possibilities of Sandy following through on her threats of killing me and my children were too real. She behaved like someone who was insane. With a stalker you don't know how crazy they are and what they are capable of doing.

The bodyguards told us a number of times that they saw her coming up the street to our house. Sometimes she drove and sometimes she was walking in the middle of the night. At least one of those times she was about to hop over the fence, but she saw them and ran off.

I could tell by her many terrible, threatening phone calls each day that she was getting worse. We had called her husband to ask him to do something to stop her before we had to get the restraining order, but he told us he was at the end of his rope with her too. She was frightening him and their son and her mother as well. I believed him. She had turned from a sweet, shy, young woman to someone who acted as though she was demon possessed and living entirely on the dark side.

I felt she was too crazy to be rational, and it was too expensive to maintain protection. Soon she would figure out she could come into our backyard from the neighbor's house just below us in the back where the bodyguards couldn't see her. She wasn't stupid. She was determined. She believed I was the only one who could help her, and nothing was going to stand in her way. If I would not help her, she would punish me.

We couldn't take a chance. So we put our house on the market, and it sold immediately with five offers and a bidding war because we were in a very popular area and people loved the house. I believed it was the Lord's doing to help us sell it so quickly. We moved quietly and secretly to another town right away and left no forwarding address. We found a house quickly because we had seen it the year before and thought it would fit our needs perfectly. It became miraculously available again.

After we moved, I was still fearful Sandy would find out where we went. I had to tell my children what had happened. I hadn't told them anything about it because I didn't want them to live in fear the way I was, but now I told them to tell me if they ever saw her. When we moved, I stopped going to all the places I formerly did and found new places to go instead.

It was the most frightening time in my life as a believer, and I knew that there was really no way out of this situation unless God did a miracle. We prayed that He would act on our behalf and save us from the enemy, who was working through her to torment us. We prayed fervently that He would take her out of our lives to someplace where she could find help.

Just when we thought she couldn't get any worse, her husband and mother had her committed to a mental hospital a few hours south of us in one of the beach towns. After that, we entered into a time of much-needed peace. I started new prayer groups in our home, and we could feel God's peace, blessings, and purpose in our lives because of them.

# 20

# Moving to the Promised Land

M ichael had been very changeable after we were married. It became
obvious that he had an anger problem, and it always manifested
toward me when I least expected it. In the beginning it hurt me
because he could be cruel and loud with his words, and every time he exploded
it felt as though I were being slapped in the face and put in the closet by my
mother. It caused me to withdraw from him and steel myself for self-protection.
This made him even angrier.

I never saw an inkling of his anger before we were married. I clearly realized
he struggled with depression and anxiety, but I understood those emotions.
I'd suffered a lifetime with them and thought we could work through those
things together. But expressing anger toward someone was not something I did,
although I saw it probably was a more advantageous negative emotion to have,
because apparently you could take your anger out on other people instead of
focusing inward and doing destructive things to yourself, as I did.

I learned that the reason Michael's mother had been so hard on him was that
she expected him to be a doctor or lawyer or some kind of professional with a
secure job. Their Armenian family had been victims of the barbarous slaughter
of Armenians by the Turks. Armenia was the first Christian nation, and their

enemies were anti-Christian. Michael's maternal grandmother witnessed the brutal murder of her husband and watched as each of her two young daughters were killed in front of her. She escaped into the forest and wandered the fields eating grass until someone found her and took her in. She left Armenia and traveled through Europe until she was able to get on a boat to America. She eventually married again and had three children, one of whom was Michael's mother.

Persecuted people can never forget the past and will do whatever it takes to see it is never repeated, which explains why Michael's mother was so strict with him, holding him to a standard he couldn't reach. That's because no one knew back then that he was dyslexic, or even what dyslexia was, which is the reason he struggled so in school. His parents thought he was just being rebellious. I came to believe those two situations became the root of Michael's anger.

Dyslexic people have a brilliant side to them. They have certain abilities that most people without dyslexia do not have. They can succeed at anything other people do, but they don't learn in the way most schools teach. They approach learning differently. When allowed to learn the way they do it best, they excel and thrive. Michael had genius abilities as a musician that came naturally to him. He didn't even have to study music, he just did it. His parents gave him accordion lessons when he was four, and he took it from there. He was destined for great things, but he had to push back against a wall of parental resistance and mutual frustration.

Michael started flying back and forth from L.A. to Nashville to produce Amy Grant and a number of other artists there. He loved Nashville and contrasted it with the concerns we had about raising teenagers in Los Angeles at that time. That city was dangerous, and drive-by shootings were rampant. He decided we should move to Nashville, so I went with him on his next trip to see the town, meet the people he knew, and look at some houses.

The problem was that he acted like a dictator and not like someone who had prayed about this move and heard God's direction for our lives. He was loveless and angry each time we saw a house and I didn't think it was the right one for us. Rather than discuss it in a civilized way, he became belligerent. I could see he was not being led by the Spirit, but by the flesh, and decided then I was not about to give up the security of everything I loved—my family, church, pastors, counselors, close friends, and prayer partners—to move clear across the country with someone as mean spirited as he was. I was afraid he would be completely unrestrained in his anger. It sounded like a nightmare.

A friend helped Michael realize that I didn't respond favorably to angry badgering, so he backed off the attacks and decided to pray that if this move was truly from God, I would hear the Lord speak to my heart about it.

I fasted and prayed about the move a number of times and told God I would do whatever *He* wanted me to do. I just had to know it was from *Him*.

Amy Grant and her husband were invited to Camp David for a special gathering of high-ranking officials of the United States, including the president and first lady, vice president, the cabinet, and many governors. She asked Michael and me to come along so he could play the piano for her. At Camp David, we were escorted to our separate cottages and then to meet with the president and first lady in their quarters. We had dinner with them the night we arrived, and the next morning, at the Sunday service in the chapel, Amy and her husband sang and Michael accompanied them.

Afterward we had a wonderful lunch with all of the government officials, at which time I was able to sit on the right side of the president, who, along with the first lady, were as gracious as any people I have ever met.

Once we were on the plane back to Amy's house, where Michael and I were spending the night before flying back to L.A., I thought about our whirlwind visit. *I have never felt so safe in my entire life as I did in that short time at Camp David. There was no threat of darkness there. And it was wonderful to not have to think about all the things I fear in L.A., where the dangers are very real, present, clear, and all around us.*

At that time in Los Angeles there was no place safe. It didn't matter what neighborhood you lived in. The contrast was stark.

While on the plane, I suffered from severe motion sickness. I have always been prone to that, but this time I had no medicine with me to treat it as I usually do. Thank God I did not throw up, as I have done in the past. However, on the drive from the airport to Amy's house in her car, I did have to ask Amy's husband to pull over to the side of the road for that purpose. I felt very embarrassed about it but was grateful to God that nothing happened in the car.

Once we were back at Amy's house I excused myself and went upstairs to our guest bedroom to lay flat on the bed in order to recover before dinner. As I was lying there, I heard from the Lord as clearly as I have ever heard anything from Him in my life. He impressed upon my heart these words, "You are to move here. Find your house and move as soon as possible, even if your house in L.A. has not been sold. My plans for you and Michael are here."

It wasn't at all what I was expecting. And I wasn't in the midst of praying about it at that moment. It was out of the blue—to me. Yet not in God's eyes. The next day we flew home and put our house on the market as soon as we could. Michael had to fly back and forth to Nashville to do more of Amy's record, and in that time he found a house for us. I didn't even have time to fly back and look at the house because as we prayed about this move together, we understood more and more the urgency to move right away. I kept feeling as if there might be a great disaster—like an earthquake—and we needed to be out of there before it happened.

Everything transpired quickly as we made plans to move. We had been in that house in Northridge for four years, and in that time we'd had peace there, but I could never get out of my spirit the sense that there was a dark and evil spirit around us. I constantly prayed that God would push it back and protect us.

Less than three weeks before we were to move, someone who knew Sandy, my stalker, and her husband and mother, and was aware of what had happened to me regarding her, called to tell me that the mental hospital was releasing Sandy within the week. A cold feeling of fear went up my spine. I envisioned us moving all the way across the country and into our house in Nashville and then seeing her peeping through a window at me and my children. It horrified me to think we might never be free of her.

I knew only God could protect us, so I prayed again that He would keep Sandy out of our lives. I prayed she would get well and concentrate on her family, and that we could make this move across the country before she could get to us. I prayed she would lose the desire to find us. I interceded for her complete healing, as I always had, but I had no reassurance that it had happened yet. In fact, I was told her husband had divorced her and didn't want to have anything to do with her. She wasn't coming back to live with him, wherever he and their son were at that time. I didn't want to know too much about their whereabouts, so I never inquired.

We thought it was best that as few people as possible knew about our move. It made me feel uneasy that even this person I was talking to knew the story, but she seemed to be on our side and was trying to warn us. I told no one the exact location where we were moving to, except for close family members. I told our friends that I would inform them once we arrived at our new home. I wanted them to be able to say they didn't know my address in case anyone inquired.

I couldn't believe Sandy was getting out of the mental hospital just days before we were to move. I didn't have peace that she was fine, especially when I had heard that her family didn't feel she was well enough to be released. I wanted to make this move across the country *before* she got out. But the day after she was released, I heard she had stayed down near the mental institution because she had met a boyfriend. I felt bad for him because I doubted if he had any clue about what he was getting into.

The day before the moving vans were to come to pick up our furniture, the same person called and told me Sandy had been murdered. Her body had been found on the beach down near the mental hospital. She had apparently been killed and then thrown over the cliff right above the beach where her body was found. I was told the boyfriend was a prime suspect, but I don't know whatever came of that. I didn't want to be close to that situation in any way, so I never asked about it.

When I heard she had been killed, I had mixed feelings. I cried for her family and especially her son. But I felt undeniable relief as well, because I would never have to worry about her stalking me or my family again. I don't believe her death was God's answer to my prayer. I believe she got crazy with someone who couldn't deal with her craziness.

It saddened me to leave Los Angeles because I had prayed so much for the people there, and I felt God's heart of love for them and His desire that they would come to know Him and His ways. It saddened me even more to leave our church and our pastor and friends. It was where I finally found hope for my life and my future. It was where I came out of darkness and met the One True Light. It was where I got rid of tormenting negative emotions and found amazing joy and peace. It was where I experienced the powerful presence and love of God that transformed my life. It was where I began to hear the voice of the Holy Spirit guiding me day by day. But it was God's Spirit leading us to leave the house we loved as soon as possible and not even wait for it to sell—which was against the advice of all others.

Los Angeles was also where my father and sister and her husband and children lived. How could I leave them? I prayed continually about that and talked with Michael about my concerns regarding them. We decided to ask them to come with us. My dad had been living with us for the past four years in his own special wing of our house. He moved in when we moved there because we had plenty of room for him to have privacy, yet he could easily join the rest of the family. It was a great arrangement for all of us. So we asked him to move with us, and he said yes immediately.

Next we asked my sister, who for the past year had been working for us on a part-time basis while she recovered from a work-related injury that happened where she was previously employed. She had been traveling an hour each way in rush-hour traffic to a job she didn't like. We offered her full-time employment running our office if she and her family would move with us. She had done such a great job working part-time for us that we wanted her to take over that job completely in Tennessee. She could live just a few miles from us with better pay and no traffic. She said she wanted to do that but needed to discuss it with her husband, Lou, and see what he thought about it.

They called soon after that and said, "Yes, we will come with you."

My sister's house sold right away, so I flew with her to Nashville and we found a house and she bought it without her husband having seen it. Our houses were in the same suburb. It was springtime and everything was in full bloom, and we agreed that we had never seen any place more beautiful. It happened to be Easter weekend, and Amy Grant and her family invited us to spend Easter Sunday lunch with them at her mother and father's house. They made us feel completely welcome and their graciousness touched us deeply. We've never forgotten that much-needed kindness.

These were life-altering moves for all of us—especially our children—and we knew that. But we were all ready to leave behind the stresses of Los Angeles. It would be like escaping out of Egypt and into the Promised Land.

Or so I thought.

# 21

# Ending Up in the Wilderness

～～

The move turned out to be much harder than we all anticipated. First of all, everything seemed foreign to us in Tennessee. They even spoke another language there—at least it seemed so in the beginning. We decided we could only ask someone to repeat something three times, because after that it seemed rude.

Even though our life in California was not perfect, at least we knew how to live there. Los Angeles is on a fairly flat grid except for a few hills. In Nashville there is no flat. It's all hills. And once when I inquired of a stranger whether I should go north on a specific road to get where I was going, he laughed and said, "There is no north, south, east, or west in Nashville. In fact, some of these streets can run all four of those directions."

I found out how true that was. Many streets not only change directions, they also change names every few miles as well. And when you ask for directions, people don't use words like "north" or "south" or specific numbers or even street names because there aren't always street signs to indicate them. They would say something like, "Go down this road here and turn right after you pass a field of cows. When you see a red truck parked on the left, take the next right, and once you pass where the Hill Market used to be, take a left."

Cows? What if they are in another field that day? A red truck? What if someone is driving it and it's gone? Where this market *used to be*?

I know this sounds like a minor thing, but because I have always had a good sense of direction, it was a big thing to be lost for most of my first year in this new place. We didn't have GPS then. We had maps, and many streets weren't on them.

In Los Angeles you know which way is north because you always know where the ocean is. If the ocean is on the left, you are going north. And that was another thing. There was no ocean to go to whenever I wanted. In L.A., we could always get to the beach in about 30 minutes if it wasn't rush hour. (In about four hours if it was.) Never mind that the only time it wasn't "rush hour" was between 11:00 at night and 4:00 in the morning. And never mind that we were usually too busy to go to the beach anyway. It was just comforting to know it was there if we wanted it. I had lived most of my life close to the beach, and I had separation anxiety when we moved to where the nearest beach is at least an eight-hour drive and required a major time and money investment. No matter what anyone says, lakes are not the same.

When we arrived in Nashville, we were extremely cautious and overly suspicious. When getting out of the car at the grocery store in Nashville, I found myself looking suspiciously around the parking lot for anyone with a gun. Come to find out later, probably everyone in the parking lot, as well as in the store, had one. But they had them legally and with permits to carry them, and they had them for protection and not for shooting innocent people in order to get into a gang. And that was a significant difference.

In the months before we left Los Angeles, a woman was shot and killed as she was about to enter the grocery store near our house—the one we often went to. This was at 10:00 on a weekday morning. People were being shot and killed while driving on the freeway, so I was afraid for my children's lives when my son drove my daughter to church youth group on Wednesday nights. A close friend of ours was shot in front of his house in broad daylight as he went to retrieve mail from his curbside mailbox. These all proved to be situations of gang-initiation violence. In order to become a member of a gang, the prospective member had to kill someone.

In Franklin, Tennessee, on a late afternoon when it was just about dark, I was driving home on a two-lane winding road and my car had a flat tire. I pulled to the side of the road to call the Auto Club to come and help me, but I had no idea how to tell them where I was. Somewhere off Highway 100, near a field of cows, past a red truck, and just before where Hill Market used to be? Actually, looking back, I think they would have known exactly where I was, but I didn't get to make that call because two men in a pickup pulled up behind me, got out of their truck, and walked up to my driver's-side window.

*I am going to die right here,* I thought. *I cannot believe I left the gang violence of L.A. to be shot to death at the side of a road in Nashville and my body hidden in the thick forest on either side.*

I rolled down my window to plead for my life, and one of the men said, "Good evening, ma'am. We'll change that tire for you."

"You will?" I exclaimed in disbelief.

"Sure. Pop your trunk," he said, and they proceeded to jack up the car and change the tire. I got out to watch as they quickly took care of everything. I was beyond grateful. I took money out of my purse to offer to them, fully intending to pay them well for their services, but they refused and seemed surprised that I would even think they would accept any payment.

Their attitude, I came to realize, was indicative of the people there. They were always kind and willing to help anyone in need. And their kindness was real. I had heard Tennessee called the Volunteer State, but I didn't really know the extent of it. How does an entire state volunteer? They do it person by person, situation by situation, day after day. It is in them to do no less. I was amazed.

When we arrived in Nashville, it was summer and beastly hot and humid. We were told it was the worst heat wave in a hundred years. And our air-conditioning was not working. We were drenched at 8:00 in the morning when we opened the doors for the moving vans. It was evident that the movers also hated that our air-conditioning didn't work. We had heat in Los Angeles too, but it was dry heat. Very different. And we immediately made the comparison.

Not only that, but the big bedroom and private bathroom we were having built for my dad had the outside wall missing. There was just a thick plastic sheet nailed to the wood frame. A minor detail, perhaps, for people in Tennessee who don't live in fear, but a major issue for anyone from L.A. We called my Aunt Jean's house, where my dad was staying until we were moved in, and told him he needed to wait a couple more weeks until we got that wall finished. He was in his late seventies and not up to the brutal heat.

The summer heat finally ended, and fall arrived. The autumn leaves were so beautiful that they stunned us. And the autumn rainstorms rattled our bones. We had never heard thunder as loud or as overwhelming as that. But afterward the green in the lawn and trees was breathtaking. By Halloween morning the first snowstorm showed up. It was soon followed by what we were told was "the worst ice storm in decades." We didn't even know what an ice storm was.

The ice storm was so powerful that the next morning when we got up, everything in our outside world was covered in glistening ice. Every tree limb, branch, and leaf was fully covered, as was every shrub, fence post, road, and doorstep. Nothing but white, shining ice. It was stunningly beautiful, like a fairyland. The town was iced in, and so were we and all of our neighbors. The fallen trees were countless. They had toppled onto roads, so even if we could have gotten out of our driveway, we couldn't have gone anywhere. They fell on power lines and knocked out nearly everyone's power.

We didn't have a generator. When our electricity went out, so did our heat. All we had for warmth was a fireplace in our kitchen, but it was so cold we had to stay within a couple feet of it to be even a little warm. We didn't have down comforters or warm pajamas. We had light, California blankets and clothes that were warm for L.A. We were all freezing and had to cook food over the fire in the fireplace. We were totally unprepared.

Once we could get out, Amy Grant asked us to come stay at her house until our power was restored. The hotels were without power too. And the ones that weren't were filled to overflowing. We gladly accepted Amy's offer. When we arrived at her home, every room in her house was filled with people who were staying there for the same reason.

Once we were able to go back home, Michael and I were lying in bed early one morning talking about all that needed to be done to repair the house, and I said, "At least the worst is over. I mean, what else could happen?"

My advice to anyone is to never say those words. It sounds too confident. Too much like a question in search of an answer. Because the second after I said that, we heard a huge explosion up above our living room followed by a giant cracking sound. And then almost immediately it was snowing something pink all over the inside of the house. We jumped up and ran upstairs to find out what happened. The ceiling in my daughter's bedroom had caved in to the floor. Thank God, she was with my sister and wasn't sleeping there that night.

It took a long time for the power to come back on. But when we finally got out and to the store, it looked like a war zone.

Everyone pitched in and helped everyone else. Even when, years later, there was a deluge of rain that destroyed countless buildings and homes in the Nashville area, no one sent the National Guard to help because the people of Tennessee helped anyone who needed it. Franklin Graham came with his enormous organization—Samaritan's Purse, one of the greatest volunteer organizations ever—and organized crews in town to help tear down damaged property, clear it out, spray for mold, and then rebuild it. My son helped with all of that. I wondered when I would see the people of Tennessee not be kind and helpful, but I never have. They are always that way.

Still, each one of us had to come to terms with how different everything was in Tennessee and deal with it. I felt I had left Egypt for the Promised Land and somehow ended up in the wilderness. That is not at all a judgment on the good people of Los Angeles or Tennessee. It was my own personal experience.

My husband and children had a hard adjustment as well. We all felt out of place, as if we didn't belong. We wondered, *Did we make a mistake? Did we really hear God? Is He putting us out to pasture? Is there really a future here? Will we ever feel at home, that we belong in this place?* But I knew without doubt it was God who called us and made everything possible.

Even though Nashville has more churches than just about anyplace else in the country, and we attended quite a few, no place was like our church in Los

Angeles and we missed it. And that was the problem. In this wilderness journey, we all had to let go of everything we craved about Los Angeles and learn to crave only the presence of God with us where we were. We learned that He wanted our full attention, because the wilderness is where He prepares us for the future He has for us. And we had to learn that we can't receive all He has for us if we are not walking closely with Him. That's because He wants to take us to places we cannot get to without Him enabling us to do so.

The wilderness experience is not about a place as much as it is the condition of our heart.

God takes us into a wilderness situation when He wants to get Egypt out of our heart.

I had a lot of Egypt in my heart. I craved things and experiences from L.A. and God wanted all of that gone. To illustrate the condition of my heart, I developed resentment toward my husband and God for leading me to a place where I was stripped of everything. I could maybe have handled it better if I was in my thirties or forties, but I had turned fifty before we moved, and it is hard to leave everything familiar to you at that age. I felt more and more as if my life was over. But the truth was, a new and wonderful period of my life was just beginning. I just couldn't see that at the time.

I knew my children were far safer in Tennessee, even though the transition was at the worst time in their lives. My son started his senior year in high school in Nashville, a time when students have already made their friends and were not about to make new friends with a stranger from a foreign land such as L.A. And my daughter was starting middle school, where cliques of longtime friends are the most entrenched. I thanked God my sister's daughter was the same age as my daughter, and even though they didn't attend the same school for more than one year, they spent nearly every weekend together. Still, it was a hard transition for every member of both of our families.

Michael and I wondered what was going to happen next. In just two short months we would find out.

# 22

# The Giant Shake-Up

We moved to Tennessee at the end of June 1993. Just over two months later, in September of that year, about two blocks from our former Northridge home, the pretty young woman who had handled our accounting at our business office in L.A.—whom we had known well for a number of years—was in her car with her nine-year-old son, picking up her young teenage daughter from a Bible study at the house of one of our former neighbors. Two men pulled up behind her car and one walked up to the driver's-side window and pointed a gun at her. He demanded her purse and briefcase, which she quickly gave to him without any argument. But he shot her anyway in front of her terrified son, and she died immediately. Her daughter came running out of the house to see that her mother had been killed. It devastated her children and husband. It grieved all of us, and it violently shook everyone who lived in the area.

I couldn't even imagine the depth of our fright if we had still been living there at the time. It was something I always feared, because this kind of deadly crime had moved closer into our nice, quiet town.

After that, it was discovered that a child pornography ring was operating nearby under everyone's noses in a place no one would suspect. I had always felt there was something evil around, but I couldn't pinpoint it. I never let my children play in the front yard—which had a security fence with electric gates. If they went outside, it was in the backyard that had a ten-foot-high brick fence all around it. Without a tall ladder, no one could see over it. That sense of evil grew in me as time went on. I know now it was God's warning to me.

With the turning of the calendar into 1994, we had weathered the heat wave, the ice storm, and now would begin to find a settling peace. But on January 17, 1994, we turned on the television in the morning and saw that a 6.7 magnitude earthquake had hit Los Angeles at 4:30 that morning. We saw scenes that looked very familiar and found out the epicenter was in Northridge—the place we had lived before we moved to Tennessee.

Caltech said it was "the strongest ground motion ever instrumentally recorded in an urban setting in North America"[1] at that time. The earthquake impacted more than 2,500 square miles and 50 cities. There were 57 deaths, 12,000 injuries, 114,000 people left homeless, 100 major alarm fires, and 449,000 homes and apartments destroyed. It was the costliest natural disaster to have occurred in the United States. Seven major freeway bridges collapsed, and 212 were damaged so badly that they could not be traveled on for some time. We found out that our house in Northridge was red-tagged, meaning that it was damaged so badly that it was too dangerous to even enter, so the city made it unlawful to do so.

That earthquake was certainly stronger than any I had ever experienced, and I thanked God we weren't there when it happened. But I worried about all of our friends and neighbors.

I instantly remembered God prompting my heart that we were to leave Northridge right away whether our house there sold or not, which was a financially risky thing to do. And we had been waiting month after month for it to sell after we moved. It was unsustainable to pay mortgages and utility bills and upkeep on two houses. It strained our finances to the point that we didn't know how much longer we could last.

But when I saw the devastation in Northridge, I thanked God that we listened. We saw on television a two-story apartment building, not more than about ten blocks from our house, that used to be a three-story building until the second floor collapsed onto the first floor, killing almost everyone inside that floor. I immediately thought of my terror when I lived in that ground-floor apartment of the three-story apartment building in Studio City and the terror I felt knowing it could collapse on me. That was more than two decades earlier. The television news was focused on this particular apartment because people living on that ground floor had been killed, but some were still unaccounted for. I shuddered to think how these people must have felt.

Once the aftershocks stopped, my children and I flew back to view the damage in our former home and see if anything was salvageable. But it was so damaged from the foundation up that it seemed impossible it could ever be repaired. We cried looking at it and thinking about what it would have been like had we been there. My children may have survived if they had stayed in their beds, but I am not sure my husband or I would have. The damage was devastating.

We signed papers to have the property sold to land barons who saw that it would one day be valuable again. We'd paid a lot for earthquake insurance, but apparently had not read the fine print that said the policy only paid for what the house was worth at the time of the earthquake. The house itself was not worth nearly as much as we had paid for it—and no one knew if it could ever be rebuilt because the foundation was wavy, lifting up as much as 15 inches in many areas. How could it ever be repaired and who would buy it? So the insurance gave us 50 percent of what we paid for it. Those two things—the sale of the land and half of what we'd paid for it—saved us from ruin. At least we were released from the financial burden of payments on something that was no longer viable as a home. We were grateful we hadn't been there when it happened because we would have lost everything *in* the house and possibly our lives as well. And that explained why it didn't sell. God kept anyone from being in that house when this disaster occurred.

After that, none of us complained anymore about leaving L.A. and having a hard time adjusting in Tennessee. We didn't question God about whether it was really His plan for us. Having one problem after another didn't mean we were out of the will of God.

Everyone we knew who had been in the earthquake, including our pastors, said it was the most violent and frightening earthquake they had ever experienced. It wasn't the swaying, side-to-side kind of earthquake we all had previously been in. It was a violent, straight, up-and-down slamming motion that made it impossible to move to a safer place. I could see clearly the terror on their faces when they described it to me in person. And I could hear in their voices how traumatic it was when they described it to me in vivid detail over the phone.

Some people we knew had homes as badly damaged as ours, but they also lost nearly everything inside. They packed up what they could and moved away. Some of them came to Tennessee where we were. Many people just walked away from their homes and everything in them that was not salvageable. It was heartbreaking. But we didn't know anyone who died or had been injured in the quake, and we were all grateful to God for that miracle.

While we had not lived through the physical shaking, this giant earthquake shook us up in our mind, soul, and spirit. It was clear that God had rescued us from what would have been a catastrophic situation had we been there sleeping in our beds that night. If we had tried to run outside, even if we could possibly have gotten there, we would have met the large roof falling in on the front porch and the three tall, brick chimneys falling down just outside the glass living room door, making a crater in the cement and brick patio. And the falling of the two-story wall of glass on the outside wall of our bedroom where the door to the outside was, as well as the crashing down of the two-story brick fireplace in the bedroom—both of which fell where the bed would have been had we been there—would have been disastrous. We were all grateful to God that He had moved us out of that house. He was saving us, and I had been complaining about how He was doing it.

We were all now curious to see what God had for each of us in Tennessee. I was convinced more than ever that we couldn't make it through life without constant abiding, fervent, ongoing prayer. I had known that already, but now it had been proven to me beyond all doubt. I never again questioned whether I could skip a day of praying.

I knew I could not.

# 23

# The Powerful Turnaround

With every passing day after the move—especially after these disasters—I spent more time praying than ever before. There were fervent prayers for my husband and children. I could see they were each struggling in their own way as they adjusted to their new life. We had left all that was familiar to go where, unexpectedly, nothing seemed familiar. Not that this was a bad thing—just very, very different. We missed our many longtime friends and, although the new acquaintances in our new land were amazingly nice and kind, it was harder to get to know people well.

Los Angeles is a melting pot of all different kinds of cultures, races, and colors. You didn't notice when someone was different because everyone was different. And that was probably the exact thing that was off-putting to the good people of our new land. And I understood that.

Gradually, over the following year, many old friends from L.A. moved near us in Tennessee. Some of them had lost their homes in the earthquake. But none of us had gotten together before the move and said, "Let's all move together." God had put this on each of our hearts separately.

My close friend, Roz, was the only one—except for family—with whom my husband and I had talked about moving to Tennessee. And that's because we were longtime prayer partners and prayed much about it together. We were quite surprised that God had put it on each of our hearts at the same time. We sought our pastor's counsel on the move, and Pastor Jack—never one to try to keep people in his church by counseling that they couldn't leave—agreed it was the Lord's leading. He always prepared people to be sent all over the nation and the world to wherever God would lead them. So he and the other pastors prayed for us in one of the Sunday morning services to be sent from the church with God's blessing.

Once we left L.A., I missed my prayer group terribly. They were strong prayer warriors, a big part of my life, and a powerful support. We had all gone to the same church, and people couldn't go to that church regularly and not learn how to pray. I deeply felt the loss of them, and I knew I needed to establish a prayer group in our home again soon.

I invited the women who had been in my group previously and who had also moved to Nashville, along with other female transplants from our new church. We knew God had brought us here, and therefore He must have a purpose in mind for us and our family members and we didn't want to miss what that was. This group of women met in my home every Tuesday morning, just like before.

One day I received a call from the police in another state telling me that Diana's husband had been killed in a car accident, and I was his son's guardian. It was devastating. Andrew and his son had spent every Christmas with us since Diana had died. I flew back west to help her son through this terrible transition. We all decided that because he would graduate from high school that year that he should stay there with close friends. After graduation he stayed with us in Tennessee until he chose the college he wanted to attend. Even though he was offered the Presidential Scholarship at Vanderbilt, he wanted to go where his good friends were going in the Pacific Northwest. I thought that was the best decision for him as well.

My prayer partners prayed us all through this tragedy and major transition.

My publishing company approached me that same year and asked if there was any subject on my heart I wanted to write about.

"Yes, I want to write a book called *The Power of a Praying Parent*," I said. "I have been thinking about it and writing notes on the subject for years. I've had prayer groups in my home to pray for children for nearly a decade. I have learned so much about how to pray, and I have seen countless answers to prayer when moms or dads regularly pray for each child. It's amazing what happens when they *keep* praying and don't give up. We've all seen God move powerfully in the life of each child for whom we have prayed."

The publisher believed in the idea and gave me the go-ahead to write it.

After I finished that book and it was published, I believed in the message of it so much—because I deeply sensed the urgency that all parents pray for their children—that I volunteered to speak at different schools to moms who wanted to start such a prayer group at their school or in their home. And they were all open to it. I never had a school or mom's group turn me down. The turnout was great at each meeting, and the praying moms totally caught the vision right away. They used my book as a tool to help guide and inspire them. Gradually, the word spread throughout the country. My publisher often told me it was the only book he had seen that sold more books each year for years. I thanked God it had been well received—just as we in my prayer group had specifically prayed.

❧

Things got worse between my husband and me after we moved to Tennessee, just as I had feared. It had started in L.A. as he grew more irritable with me and the children. We all walked on eggshells around him, hoping to avoid his anger directed at us, and it became too stressful to be healthy. In Tennessee it grew unbearable, and I couldn't take it anymore.

One Saturday when Michael was gone on a golf trip with his friends, and my children were also gone spending the day with their friends, I sat on my bed hugging my Bible and poured out my heart to God about my marriage.

For years I had been praying my favorite three-word prayer for my husband, which was, "Change him, Lord!" *Why is God either not hearing my prayer or refusing to answer it?* I confess I even became upset with God for giving me a husband who was verbally abusive sometimes the way my mother had been. *Haven't I suffered enough with that kind of treatment? Why did God let me marry him without showing me what he would be like?*

"Lord, I know You don't violate our will," I said. "But if Michael doesn't want to change because he is fine with the way he is, what about the rest of us? I know what You said about divorce—how You hate it, and I hate what You hate—but I feel as though I'm dying in this marriage. Help me, Lord. I can't live this way anymore, and I don't know what to do."

Because of the excellent sales of the *Praying Parent* book, I had just received a larger royalty check than I'd ever had before. I struggled mightily with the temptation to take my children and the check and leave. I could buy a small condominium and never again in my life have to be emotionally beat up by verbal abuse. Of course, I knew I would go through hell if I did that. I would have the wrath of the Christian community, so I could never write for a Christian publisher again. And how would I support the three of us? And who would still be our friends? The picture of our future became so horribly tragic that I had no peace about it. And I knew it wasn't the answer because it wasn't God's will. I could not violate that.

I cried before the Lord, confessing everything that was in my heart at that moment, and I asked Him to forgive me. "Speak to me, Lord. Help me. I am going to fast and pray today until I hear from You."

I sat there waiting upon the Lord and didn't leave that place until I heard God's voice penetrate my heart as clearly as I had ever heard Him before.

He said, "If you will lay down your desire to leave and do what I am asking you to do, I will bless you. First of all you must stop praying your favorite three-word prayer—'Change him, Lord'—and pray *My* favorite three-word prayer—'Change *me*, Lord.'"

Those words sent shockwaves through my system.

"But, Lord, I'm not the one who needs changing here. It's *him*," I said as respectfully as I could.

God invited me to reason with Him about this. "*Everyone* needs to change," He explained, "because everyone falls short of what I want them to be."

*God wants us all to become more like Him,* I realized.

"If you are willing to change," He continued, "I can use you as an instrument of deliverance for your husband. If you are willing to lay down your desire to leave and surrender to My will for your life, I will teach you to pray the way I want you to for your husband."

It actually hurt to lay down all the injustices collected from the past in our marriage and begin again as if these offensive things had never happened, but I said yes to God. There were no guarantees, but there was also no other option.

God further instructed me that in order to get my heart right toward my husband, I had to confess every unforgiving or bitter thought I had *before* I prayed each day for him. God would not hear my prayers if I didn't. The Bible says, "If I regard iniquity in my heart, the Lord will not hear."[1] My own unforgiveness, bitterness, doubt, and negative thinking were all iniquity—or sin—in God's eyes, and He wanted me to get my heart right *before* He would answer my prayers.

When my husband came home the next day, I told him what the Lord had impressed upon my heart. "Michael, God showed me that I have not been praying for you the way He wants me to, so I'm going to pray for you every day, and I want you to tell me specifically how you want me to pray."

He agreed to do that.

Each morning I asked Michael how he wanted me to pray for him, and the most amazing thing happened. He would take the time to tell me about all that was troubling him—many things I didn't even know.

Every time his anger would flare up, instead of my reacting to it, I prayed that God would show me what was causing it and help me respond in the way that I should. I asked God to take my husband's anger away and give him peace. Each time I did that, I saw his anger dissipate instead of grow in intensity. I couldn't believe my eyes. The more I prayed for him the way God wanted me to, the more changes I saw happening in him. And in *me*!

The changes happening in me came about because before I prayed for my husband, I had to make sure I had no bad feelings, thoughts, or attitudes in my heart toward him—or anyone else, for that matter. I quickly came to see how the "iniquity in my heart" had kept my prayers from being answered. I shared all of this with my prayer group, and they prayed for us each step of the way. The atmosphere of our home gradually transformed as God showed me how to pray for Michael every day.

When my publisher again asked me the following year if there was anything I wanted to write about, I said, "Yes. I want to write *The Power of a Praying Wife*." I told them what had happened and all God had taught me, but the publishing committee had concerns about how it would sell because at that time books on raising children sold far better than books on marriage. They were willing to publish it, but it had to be cross-collateralized with the *Praying Parent* book. That meant if *Praying Wife* didn't sell, they would take royalties from *Praying Parent* to offset any loss.

I was certain it was God's will that I write this book, and I knew that the heart of most women is to have their marriage not only work, but thrive and become all God wants it to be. Because my prayer group had prayed me through every book I wrote, I knew I couldn't write this book without their prayer support. It was certain to be more difficult than the rest. And it was.

I had an especially dedicated, fervently praying group of seven women who were women of the Word; who had faithful, humble, and pure hearts before God; and who wanted His will to be done in their lives and in the lives of their children and husband more than anything.

One Monday I was praying in preparation before our Tuesday morning prayer group the next day, and I felt strongly led by the Lord to pray in a certain way regarding the *Praying Wife* book that was different from how I had ever prayed for any book before. I didn't want to bring a prayer request like this to my prayer group on a whim, but I knew I wouldn't have conjured this up on my own. And God assured me with His peace that it was definitely His will.

When it came time for me to share my requests in the prayer group that morning, I said, "I have an unusual prayer request, and I believe it's from God because I wouldn't have thought of this myself. But I want you to pray with me about this and tell me if your spirit bears witness to it or not.

"My prayer request is this," I continued. "I want you to pray that this book I am writing, *The Power of a Praying Wife*, will be a breakthrough book and be taken all over the world, to every nation God would take it, and to be translated into every language God wants it translated. I know this could sound like visions of grandeur or just plain arrogance, but I come humbly before you with this request."

Without pause, everyone in the group said their spirit resonated to my request. They believed it was truly from God and that we should pray this way for the book every week—even after it was released. And so we did.

When the book came out, it was so well received that it went to number one on the Christian Bookseller Association's bestseller list. I called my publisher right away to thank him.

"Hi, Bob. I want to thank you for all your company did to cause this book to be number one on the charts. I'm so grateful."

"Oh, we didn't have anything to do with that," he humbly replied.

"You didn't?" I was shocked.

"No, only God can do that," he said firmly, and then he went on to tell me how the book's sales had increased every month since its release, even beyond *Praying Parent*'s record sales. "I've never seen anything like it."

My prayer partners and I recognized it was the Lord answering the prayers He instructed us to pray. We learned that when God wants us to pray beyond ourselves, we must listen and do what He says. He wants to do powerful things through us that cannot happen without Him.

In fact, it was an eye-opener for all of us because of what happened with that book. Where the *Praying Parent* book sold more than 3.5 million copies, the *Praying Wife* book sold more than double that. They were both translated into more than 35 different languages and sent to all the countries where people spoke those languages. God answered our prayers that the book would be taken all over the world, even beyond our dreams.

Like *Praying Parent*, *Praying Wife* sold more each year than the year before. That's because women started prayer groups with it and word of mouth spread. I commend the women who were so willing to do the difficult task of praying—especially the "Change me" prayer. It's challenging for everyone, but it accomplishes much. I knew it did miracles for us, but I didn't know how many women would do the hard work. As it turned out, millions did. And I received countless letters and emails with personal testimonies from wives of the miracles God worked in their marriages. Of course, not everyone got such a good response from their husband, because a man must have a heart that is willing to be changed by God. And not every person has that.

The book stayed at number one for 27 consecutive months, only slipping to number two when *The Power of a Praying Husband* followed two years later and replaced it as number one for one month and then *The Power of a Praying Wife* went back to number one for another 12 months. It stayed in the top 50 for 32 consecutive months and has frequently appeared in the top 50 for more than 15 years.

Only God can do all that.

After that, I wrote *The Power of a Praying Woman* to help women pray for themselves in a way that brings them closer to God in an ever-deepening walk with Him. It, too, sold millions of copies and went all over the world and was translated into many languages.

When I was approached by my publisher to write *Praying Husband*, I was concerned about how a man would receive a book written by a woman telling him how to pray for his wife. But I prayed much about it and felt led to write it from a *woman's perspective*. I took surveys of women wherever I went about how she would most like her husband to pray for her. I wanted this book to help a husband better understand his wife and her needs and to know how to pray.

In each of the chapters in that book I included a written contribution from either my husband or another godly man who prayed regularly for his wife. Men received it well, and many men started prayer groups for husbands, using the book as a guide to pray for their wives. I even received a photo of military soldiers in Iraq who were praying for their wives back home. They were each holding a *Praying Husband* book I had sent them. I was deeply touched by these men, who were remembering to pray for their wives back home even as they were putting their lives on the line for our country. That photo is one of my most cherished possessions.

After that I wrote one book after another on prayer for every age, from three years old on up. I tailored each one specifically to the needs of those God had put on my heart.

During all of this, people frequently asked me, "How do you get started writing?" "How do you organize your thoughts, notes, and time?" By this time I clearly had seven specific stages of writing that I went through. They were more humorous than scientific. I have no idea as to whether they would work for anyone else, but at one point in my life—before I wrote my second book decades ago—I read every book I could find on writing. Each one helped me tremendously. I had also taken a creative writing course in college that was the best, and I learned more from that one young female professor than anyone else. I never forgot all she taught me. She didn't teach me my seven stages of writing, however. I don't want to blame this system on her. Nor did I learn it from anyone else. But this is the way it has always worked for me. Because so many people have asked for it, I have included it here.

# Stormie Omartian's Seven Stages of Writing

In the beginning, God gives me a vision for a book, and I pray about it until I am certain it's His will and He approves of it. At that point, I understand what the book is to be about even if I don't know all of the specifics. It's usually something God has taught me through His Word or what I have experienced—usually both. I ask God to reveal to me all I need to know as I seek Him every day. In each one of these stages I go entirely through the book, from what I believe is the beginning to what I believe is the end, even though that could change at any time.

## Stage 1. "The Jumbled Mess"

This stage consists of all the research I have collected for months or even years before I ever sit down to formally write it. This stage includes everything God has put on my heart about the book—my thoughts, understanding, ideas, notes, personal experiences, stories, examples, illustrations, or anything He has revealed to me regarding it. I also collect Bible content until I believe I have a solid scriptural foundation upon which to base the book. If I don't have a biblical foundation for it, I won't do it.

## Stage 2. "Establishing Order in the Midst of Chaos"

This stage takes "the jumbled mess" of notes and research I have accumulated and puts it in order. That means constructing the Contents page and filing everything under one of those categories. I don't move on until I have this road map that will get me where I need to go. Even if it is rough and may change later, everything I have gathered must go somewhere in the chapters I have listed. I make a title page for each chapter and every note of research goes in one of those chapters. Establishing the Contents page takes a great deal of time and prayer.

### Stage 3. "What Was I Thinking When I Signed That Contract?"

It all seemed so clear in the beginning, but now as I start to write, it's overwhelming. I have doubts about my ability to pull it all together. And this, I have found out, is a good thing. That's because I must fully realize I cannot do this without God. In fact, I am never allowed to think for even a moment that I can pull this off without Him. And believe me, I don't.

### Stage 4. "God, I Need a Miracle"

This is when I fully recognize that the only way this will get done right is if God does it. Just because I have the vision for the book in the beginning—which comes from Him anyway—doesn't mean I can carry it out on my own strength. I realize how dependent I am on God. In fact, I'm certain that I not only need His help, I need His miracle. This stage includes being prostrate before God and in fervent prayer through every bit of writing

### Stage 5. "This Could Work"

A glimmer of hope begins to appear as God answers my prayers, and I more clearly see the purpose and promise in this book. I believe He will use it to touch the hearts of readers everywhere, so I go through each chapter until I see the hope, vision, and purpose for what each chapter is to communicate.

### Stage 6. "Why Would Someone Want to Read This Book?"

When I go through the book the sixth time, I have to determine what's in it for the reader in each chapter. Why would they want to spend their time reading this book? How does it touch the reader and make a difference in their life? What are the personal stories and heartbeat of the book? How can it flow more smoothly? I look for every possible flaw that needs to be changed. That's hard to do and why authors need editors. I am too close to see everything. I know what word is supposed to be where and my mind can easily put it there when I am reading whether it's actually there or not.

### Stage 7. "I Don't Know if the Book Is Done, but *I'm* Done"

When I go through the book for the seventh time, I see if anything is missing or needs to be changed. When I cannot go any further—when my brain is fried and I just can't read through it again—there is a time to simply leave it alone. I can always find something to change, but that may not be a good thing. When the changes I make at midnight—trying to perfect it—don't look as good in the morning, that's when it's time to stop.

That's when I don't know if the book is done, but *I'm* done.

Now, more than 50 books later, with more than 34 million copies sold worldwide, I know with certainty that none of this could ever have happened without God. And I am more dependent on Him now than ever before. My husband and I have been married more than 42 years, and my prayer partners are still going strong. Everything has turned around for good.

Only God can do all that!

24

# A Near-Death Experience

After the *Praying Wife* and *Praying Woman* books came out, and while I was in the midst of writing *Praying Husband*, I nearly died. In fact, the surgeon who operated on me said, "You were so close to death. Another hour and I couldn't have saved you."

I had been feeling badly in my abdominal area for some time. Too often, I had such pain and nausea after a meal that I couldn't move. Each time it became unbearable, my husband had to take me to the emergency room for tests and treatment. I ended up going to different doctors, specialists, gastroenterologists, and various hospitals, always praying that someone somewhere could find something. They tried numerous examinations and procedures on me in case something might work, but nothing did.

One Sunday night I experienced a lot of pain and nausea, but because I had an appointment with a gastroenterologist early the next morning, I decided I would stay home as long as I could bear it and be in my own bed rather than spend all night in the ER waiting to be seen and then being told once again that they couldn't find anything wrong with me. I didn't understand how I could be in that much pain and yet the doctors and technicians consistently found nothing wrong.

Michael went up to the guest room to sleep so at least one of us would feel rested the next morning. About midnight the pain got much worse. I was lying on my side hugging my stomach when I felt something explode in my lower abdominal area. That pain was more excruciating than any I had ever experienced—including childbirth. I knew I could die from it and had to get to the hospital immediately, yet I was paralyzed by the pain. I couldn't even extend my arm the 18 inches or so to reach the phone to call my husband. I waited a few seconds to see if the pain would subside enough for me to move, but it was unrelenting. So I let myself fall over on the bedside table where the phone was, and I pushed the intercom button and cried, "Michael, help me! I have to get to the emergency room right now!"

He came running down the stairs, and I told him I had felt something explode in my body. He asked me if he should call an ambulance and I, doubled over and barely able to talk, said one of the stupidest things I have ever said in my life. "No, I don't have time to wait for an ambulance. I have to get there now."

I would regret that decision and pay for it for years to come—perhaps even for the rest of my life.

Michael carried me to the car while I was doubled over and crying in pain. All I could pray was, "Help me, Jesus."

At the hospital everything moved in slow motion. The emergency room was packed. I told them I thought my appendix had ruptured because I felt something in that area explode. They could see I was in excruciating pain, but they couldn't give me anything for it because they didn't know what was wrong with me. They did painful test after test, and each one revealed nothing to them.

I could feel life going out of my body, and I knew I wouldn't survive if someone didn't do something soon. I had been in the ER for a couple hours before Suzy and Roz came in to pray for me. Michael and I had, of course, been praying too, but the reinforcement of their prayers was beyond comforting. They called people all over the country who knew me to pray for a miracle.

I asked the Lord, *Is this my time to die? Am I going home to be with You?* But He gave me assurance that this was not my time.

I begged every medical person who came in to the area where I was to help me, but they ignored my pleas. Then they decided that because they couldn't find anything wrong with me, they were going to send me home and I could just keep my appointment to see the gastroenterologist at 9:00 that morning. Michael and I both knew I couldn't be moved anyplace except to an operating room. In fact, my husband and sister could see I was getting weaker, so they firmly insisted that the staff come into the room to see that I had clearly turned yellow and they had to do something right then. By that time it had been about eight hours since this explosion happened in my body.

A young surgeon came to examine me, and I told him I thought my appendix had ruptured. He was the first one who believed me. He felt the area where the pain was coming from, and I nearly leapt through the ceiling. He was appalled that I had been lying there for eight hours with no help whatsoever. He ordered that I be prepped for emergency surgery immediately.

"I believe you're right about your appendix having ruptured," he said, "but if it's not that, I will do exploratory surgery to find out what *is* wrong."

I was in surgery many hours, and after I came out of the anesthetic, the surgeon came into the room where I was recovering and told me, "Your appendix definitely ruptured. In another hour I couldn't have saved you. The poison was spread everywhere, and I had to open up your abdominal wall and intestines to vacuum it out. That's why the surgery was so long. I have left a hole in your abdominal area connected to that big machine there that will suction the poison out. You can't eat or drink anything for the next ten to fourteen days until those incisions are healed enough to do so. You can still die from this, so you'll have to be connected to that machine the entire time you're here."

I could see the tube coming out of my heavily bandaged stomach and into a machine that was constantly pumping. *The hole in me must be at least an inch in diameter, the size of that tube,* I thought. It was creepy to think of an opening as big as that in my body.

I thanked the surgeon profusely and told him he was the greatest answer to prayer I'd ever had, and I knew he'd been sent by God. I never asked him if he was a believer, even though I felt he was one because of his especially kind and compassionate spirit.

My son and daughter came to see me at different times that day, and some of my close women friends organized a schedule for each one to come and help me every morning and afternoon.

Christopher had just started his senior year at his university, and Mandy had just started the new semester at her college. Both had stayed in town to go to school, so they were close by. Mandy said she wanted to come and spend every night with me from 7:00 p.m. to 7:00 a.m., even though I tried to talk her out of it. They poured fluids in me through an IV, so I was forced to get up every two hours to walk to the bathroom and then walk very slowly and painfully around the halls surrounding the large nurses' station for 30 minutes afterward in order to keep my circulation going so infection wouldn't set in. That meant I had to be unhooked from the machine that was connected to the tube in my stomach. But I had to take everything else I was hooked up to with me—the morphine pump, antibiotic drip, and the IV bag on their pole as well.

I attempted to discourage my daughter from staying the night with me because it was way too much for her to sleep in that uncomfortable chair that made down into a narrow, hard bed and be up every two hours for a half an hour of walking me to the bathroom and then around the halls, and then go back to college for classes in the morning.

"Mom," she stated emphatically. "I can't be anyplace else knowing you are suffering here alone. I *have* to be here."

It touched me deeply that she would make so great a sacrifice as that. She came every evening at 7:00 and helped me up to walk, and then she did her homework. She helped me up to walk again at 9:00 and then went to bed. She helped me up at 11:00, 1:00, 3:00, and 5:00, and then she showered and left for college classes after she walked me again at 7:00. I truly don't know how she did that every night for as long as I was in the hospital, but she kept saying to me, "Mom I can't be anyplace else." I was forever grateful.

The surgeon came in early every morning to check on me and warn me of what was happening that day. On the first morning after the surgery, he came in around 6:00 to tell me a doctor and nurses would come in to change the bandages every morning. My friend Michelle came at 9:00 to help me get up and do the walk. Just as she carefully helped me back to bed and hooked me up to the machine again—which was extremely painful when that suction started to pull everything back together—a group of about ten doctors, nurses, and interns came in for the first changing of the bandages.

Michelle stood next to me at my right shoulder, and we watched what we never imagined seeing. The doctor stripped away the bandages, which covered my entire abdominal area, and we saw that the incision was not the one-inch size I thought it was. It was close to eighteen inches long. My body fell completely open because it had not been stitched up. Everyone could see the wall of my abdominal cavity and all the dissolvable stitches where it had been internally sewn up. They explained that there were so many people in the room to see this because it was rare to have such an extensive surgery with such a giant "open wound," as they called it.

Michelle and I were not prepared to see the entirety of my insides in all their bloody rawness. It was so excruciating and shocking that when that large cavity opened up before our eyes, I know I would have collapsed if I hadn't been already lying down. One of the nurses noticed Michelle starting to pass out and assisted her out of the room.

This daily process of ripping off the bandages—and I do mean ripping—and cleaning the giant open wound was excruciating. I had a morphine drip where I could press a button and be given more medication in my vein, but there was a limit to how much I could have and so I kept it in reserve for these bandage-changing times. They gave me another pain killer at that time as well, but it was still always unbearably painful.

After ten days the surgeon said, "You're having too many daily visitors and could be exposed to a bacterial infection. You're still not out of the woods with this. You could still die. That's why I'm sending you home with three nurses who will rotate every day. They will change your bandages and suction everything out. Don't allow people to come over except for your immediate family. Your immune system has been compromised, and this can affect every organ in your body. You cannot take a chance."

"You're not going to stitch me up before I go home?" I asked in horror.

"Because of the danger of serious infection, you can't be stitched up. You will have to heal from the inside out."

"How long will that take?"

"About five or six months," he replied. I had visions of feeling that terrible and being that incapacitated the entire time. Still, I felt glad to go home because I got very little sleep in the hospital.

The best news was, however, that I did not have to take that tortuous machine with me. That had been a possibility. Instead, the visiting nurses would clean the large opening out by hand with sponges and pads, which turned out to be not as much fun as it sounds.

"You are going to have trouble with those scars," the surgeon explained further.

"That's all right. I don't care how it looks. I know you saved my life, and that's what matters."

"I don't mean that *scar*," he explained. "I am talking about the scars internally. I had to cut in so many places to vacuum out all the poison that these internal scars will definitely give you trouble in years to come."

I thought, *How bad can it be? Nothing compares to what I've already been through.*

How wrong I was. I had no idea what the future would hold for me with regard to that. It took five months before the open wound closed up. It has been fifteen years since then, and I am still dealing with the consequences of what happened and those scars.

God saved my life by bringing this wonderful, brave young doctor to the rescue. The three nurses who helped me every day at home were kind and compassionate. All of them were believers. And they didn't just rip the bandages off every day like what happened in the hospital. They could see I was allergic to the bandages they had been using, which were causing bleeding sores, so they obtained allergenic bandages for me and that made an enormous difference. They went out of their way to help me. And I prayed with them often about the problems they were having in their lives and gave them some of my books. They were like angels God had sent to help me, and I am forever grateful for each of them.

After I was home from the hospital about two or three weeks, I suddenly experienced the same painful attack all over again—the feeling I used to get before my appendix ruptured. I couldn't believe that after all I had been through, I was back where I was before and had to go to the emergency room *again*. This time, however, my gastroenterologist was on duty when I arrived. He called the best people in and said in no uncertain terms that he wanted answers. "Do not come back and tell me you cannot find anything wrong," he told them.

The technicians did what he said and found that I had about a hundred small gallstones, and they believed this was what started all of my problems in the first place. No one had found them before because they were too small for normal tests to reveal them. I had to have my gallbladder removed, but it was done through laparoscopic surgery and was not nearly the nightmare the other operation had been. Still, I was far from healed from the first surgery, so it was difficult.

If someone had been able to identify my problem properly, all of this wouldn't have happened. I wondered why it was never revealed after we had prayed so much about it, but I've learned not to question God about things like that. He knows why He allows certain situations. Probably it's to humble us from ever thinking we can live without Him for a moment. In fact, I learned that the more God allows us to be blessed, the more dependent He makes us on Him.

When we have known God and received revelation from Him, the enemy and the realm of darkness tries to subvert everything the Lord wants to do *in* us and *through* us. If we are not totally dependent on God, we won't hear His leading. When I had this near-death experience, I knew my life was entirely in God's hands. If I lived, it would be one hundred percent His doing.

✸

The recovery was very long—at least five years of putting out fires. The poison had damaged so much of my internal organs and systems that many problems had to be addressed one by one.

It also triggered physical problems and malfunctions I'd never had before.

My cholesterol, which had always been normal, went sky high. I'd always had healthy bones, but now I had osteoporosis. My hormone balance was off. My immune system had been so compromised that I caught every bug that went around. The migraines alone were so severe that it took a full 24 hours to recover from one—and I had them several times a week. And then eventually nearly every day. The allergies I had became far worse, and digestive problems were incapacitating as well. In every case, the medicine I was given by doctors for each problem interfered severely with my problematic digestive system and, in some cases we believed, contributed to the painful blockage that was caused by the scars the doctor warned me about.

From then on I was behind on every writing project because I had one physical problem after another.

My friend Sally told me about the Hotze Health and Wellness Center in Houston, and they helped me get my life back. Sally had gone there for a number of health problems, and when I saw her two weeks after she returned, I couldn't believe what a difference they had made. She looked and felt like a new person.

Although the doctors at Hotze are all medical doctors, they recognized that I couldn't handle the side-effects of certain drugs and so devised another way for those of us who cannot take the drugs—for whatever reason—to receive healing benefits. They helped me to balance my hormones, to come completely out of osteoporosis and back into having healthy bones again, to get rid of migraines and allergies, and to bring my high cholesterol down without medicine and side effects. All of this didn't happen overnight, but I began to see good results right away.

I still have dietary restrictions that will be lifelong, and there are many foods I love that I will never be able to eat again. And I'm always aware that anything I eat, or medicine I take, could trigger the blockage. I can never allow myself to get really full, or eat too many kinds of things at once. The surgery I underwent for a ruptured appendix altered my life from that point on.

One time when that blockage occurred and I was in the emergency room again, I was warned by the doctor there that I needed to get into the ER sooner because the blockage could cause a rupture and I could surely die from that. I have always kept that in my mind.

The doctor also told me that having surgery to fix the blockage would mean losing part of my small intestine and causing digestion problems for the rest of my life. I definitely want to avoid that, so I am extremely careful. I have ended up in the hospital many times with this blockage, where they either pumped my stomach for three days or gave me medicine that worked. The last time I was again experiencing excruciating pain from this blockage, we called an ambulance. I wasn't going to make the same mistake again and end up in emergency surgery or dead because I waited too long.

God has helped me to recover day by day and year by year, but when I look at that long scar, it reminds me that He saved me from death and I depend on Him for my existence every day. This experience altered my life, and I was never the same again. I was more dependent on God than ever.

Michael was supportive through it all, even though it must have been discouraging for him at times.

Then it was his turn.

# 25

# In Sickness and in Health

My husband and I vowed at our wedding to love each other in sickness and in health. The sickness part tests our true character. I am not talking about the occasional cold, flu, broken bone, sprained ankle, aching back, or headache. I am talking about the incapacitating illness or accident—the disease or infirmity that alters your life—where it requires everything you have within you to get through it mentally, physically, emotionally, spiritually, and financially. I am talking about an illness, disease, or accident that could lead to disability or death, and you don't know the final outcome at the time.

When you and your spouse are forced into total dependence on God for *any* outcome and you rise to that challenge, you both are changed for the rest of your lives. Those who survive it as a couple grow stronger together as well as individually. Those who find their refuge in the Lord grow richer and deeper in Him. Those who don't experience all that can fall apart.

As I said before, being dependent on God is a good thing. That's because He allows us to get to a place where we are so dependent on Him that He can do great things in and through us that would never be possible if *we* were in charge. In fact, *not* being dependent on God is a dangerous place to be.

When you have to depend on *God* for strength to face your situation, then anything is possible for you. If you say with faith, "I can do all things through Christ who strengthens me,"[1] you can make it through another day because it will be *His* strength that carries you. And He will make possible that which doesn't seem possible at the time. You can survive what you are facing because you have the Light of the world and His Spirit lives *in* you. That means no matter how dark the situation you are in seems to be, when you walk with Him you can never truly be in the dark. In the darkest times of our life we can always find His light in them. We take a step at a time, a day at a time, and He gives us the light we need for the step we're on. I had written a book about that, called *Just Enough Light for the Step I'm On*, and what I learned was put to the test fully in this next experience.

One morning as Michael was shaving at the sink, I saw something on his skin at the back of his knee that looked different to me. I called his attention to it, but he said it was probably a breakout of psoriasis that he gets frequently. It didn't look like that to me, but he said he would put medicine on it.

Throughout the next month it looked worse to me every time I saw it.

"Have you had that checked by the doctor yet?" I kept asking him. "Are you putting any medicine on it?"

He always replied, "I haven't been to the doctor, but I'm putting the medicine he gave me on it."

To which I always replied, "Whatever you're doing isn't working. Please go to the doctor."

It was bothering me more and more because it looked strange and unlike anything I'd ever seen.

One morning I walked into the bathroom where he was again at the sink shaving, and I couldn't help but look at his leg behind his knee. The large eruption had grown to about the size of a small grapefruit in circumference. In that large irregular circle appeared what looked like many blood blisters of various shapes and sizes, and different shades of red, pink, and purple. It appeared raw and oozing, although I didn't know if it really was or not. I didn't touch it.

"Michael! Have you really looked at this thing on the back of your leg? It looks awful. Call the dermatologist. You are going to see him today. Immediately! I mean it. Cancel whatever you're doing. This isn't like anything I've ever seen," I said emphatically. He could tell by my alarm that it was very serious, so he called the doctor and got in that day, which was a miracle in itself.

The dermatologist looked at it and said, "We need to do a biopsy right away." He called back within a day or two and said that the biopsy showed they had found cancer cells. "I am sending you to an oncologist who specializes in lymphoma."

Michael got in to see a lymphoma oncologist at Vanderbilt Hospital within a few days. "This definitely looks like lymphoma," she confirmed and ordered a number of tests, including a bone marrow test and an MRI. It took a week before the results of the tests were back. She called us into her office and said, "Michael, you have non-Hodgkin's lymphoma."

I knew exactly what that was because I was aware of many people who had died from it, including Jackie Kennedy. I knew it was deadly.

We learned that day that there were two places in the United States that had advanced, successful treatment specifically for non-Hodgkin's lymphoma at that time. One was in Houston, Texas, at MD Anderson, and the other was at Vanderbilt Hospital—20 minutes from where we lived. There was a special wing at Vanderbilt with large letters at the entrance that said simply, LYMPHOMA. The first nurse he saw there said, "If you have to have cancer, this is the one to have here."

The lymphoma specialist explained that they were taking samples of his DNA to design a chemotherapy treatment that would be the best and most effective for his body.

When it came time to go for his first chemotherapy treatment three weeks later, we, our prayer partners, and people all over the country had prayed for this day. Although we were extremely nervous, we felt the Lord's presence and peace. When we arrived at the Vanderbilt Hospital Lymphoma Center, there were a surprising number of people waiting to be called in to one of the numerous infusion rooms. When Michael was called into the small infusion room assigned to him, we felt that God's presence had gone before us just as we had prayed.

I watched as they hooked him up to various monitors and connected him intravenously to a main source of liquid drip. They then attached a number of different bags of liquid to him—each for a different kind of purpose that would prepare his body for what he was about to receive. They said they were waiting for his specifically designed chemotherapy to arrive, which was due any moment. We prayed again after we were alone because it was impossible not to.

When the specially prepared chemotherapy arrived, the person hooking it up to him came in wearing a full hazardous materials suit that covered her from head to toe. We couldn't see any part of that person at all.

I thought, *Dear Lord, if the person attaching this bag of chemotherapy liquid to my husband's IV cannot even risk getting a drop of it anywhere on her, and yet this is going into his veins, what is the risk for him?*

Michael was thinking the same thing.

The smell of the chemo was sickening to us. We had smelled it when we walked into that wing of the hospital. Room after room of people were being filled with chemotherapy for various types of lymphoma. Some people looked fairly well, but some looked thin and frail. They were lying down in a bed without the strength to sit up in a reclining chair the way Michael was. Once the chemo was being dripped into his body, the smell became much stronger.

After the chemotherapy was finished, they gave him another bag of something to drip into his veins to help him cope with the chemo they had just given him.

We were there in that infusion room a total of eight hours.

As I drove him home, we talked mostly about the person wearing the hazmat suit hooking him up to the chemotherapy drip that was now in his blood. We didn't know what to expect. I prayed it wouldn't kill him in the night. We slept in separate rooms so we wouldn't disturb each other throughout the night, but I kept waking up to go check on him, and he was always sleeping, although his breathing was unusually heavy. I could tell his body was dealing with something very serious.

The next morning I drove him back to the hospital for a strong steroid shot that affected him for days. It made his personality extremely volatile, and he would explode violently over nothing. The roller coaster continued up and down until by the beginning of the third week it finally started to calm down. Just as he began to feel better, he had to go in for the next round of chemo.

After the last infusion of chemotherapy, he started radiation on his leg—day after day of it. Again we felt God's presence with us. After the first radiation treatment, he started driving himself. We kept praying through every day, and God met us each step of the way.

We had two little longhaired Chihuahuas. One always slept near me in his own little bed. The other one always slept right next to Michael's side. When Michael started treatment, the smell of the chemo bothered the little dog so much that he wouldn't sleep near Michael at all. It was a good day when the chemo treatments were over and this little furry, faithful friend was again sleeping by his side.

It has been three years since the treatments ended, and the cancer has not returned. The oncologist said that this is a very good sign, because this deadly cancer will come back in one year if the treatment hasn't worked. She said that usually if a person is cancer-free from non-Hodgkin's lymphoma for three years, it will not come back, but if it *did* come back, they would go back and treat it again. We thank God that it has not returned, and we continue to pray it never *will*.

Michael said during all of this that what comforted him most were all the nurses at the lymphoma center who had read my books. "I feel like I'm in good hands when I hear that," he said. "If they are reading your books, they must be praying people."

❦

Those two giant life-and-death medical issues my husband and I went through gave us each a chance to prove how fully committed we were to each other. It's so important for any husband or wife to know that their spouse will be there 100 percent to see them through the tough times. It strengthens their relationship. And it did that for us.

Going through the dark times of our deadly illnesses changed both of us. We were now able to overlook insignificant problems by letting go of things that don't matter. A day that no longer involves a life-or-death situation is a good day. *But even if it does*, it's still a good day because of the Lord in us.

Bad things happen, and we don't always know why. But God works good in all situations if we continue to walk closely with Him and keep praying through them. I believe that with all my heart, even though it's not easy going through difficult things at the time, and especially if they don't turn out the way we want them to. We may go through dark times, but God will provide the light we need for the moment we're in.

I was there for Michael in sickness and in health as I vowed I would be—although I did say that if he ever had to take a strong steroid shot like that again, I was moving to a hotel until it wore off.

# 26

# A Place of Safety

Once I started speaking around the country again, many people knew what had happened and mentioned how they had prayed for me when they heard the news of my near-death experience. I was still in that serious five-year period of recovery, and it meant more than words could express to hear about their support.

During those years there were three women, each in a different state or country, and in a different year, who told me something very interesting that they felt the Lord showed them about my past. They each used exactly the same words.

The first woman who shared that particular insight surprised me.

"Thank you for sharing that with me," I replied. "I've never thought of it that way."

I kept what she had said in my mind, but I did not know her at all and had no idea what to make of something so strange to me at that time. She seemed completely sincere and had the humble and gentle spirit that those who hear from God usually have, but I had never thought of anything like that and didn't know what to make of it.

I knew the Bible said that "By the mouth of two or three witnesses every word shall be established."[1] So I prayed, "Lord, if there is anything to this, let it be confirmed by two more witnesses." I didn't hear anything like that for at least another year or two.

Then one afternoon, after speaking at a women's conference in Canada, another lady approached me and said the same thing as the first woman had—even using some of the same words. I still thought it sounded odd, and I didn't understand it at all. I thanked her for sharing that and told her of how someone else had spoken those same words to me at least a year previously.

"I'll pray and see what the Lord speaks to my heart about that," I promised.

I thought it was an interesting coincidence that two women in different countries told me the same message. Again, I asked God to show me the truth about what they said. I felt those words dismissed the damage that had been done to me in my past. I was totally unable to see what they were talking about.

About two years later I went back to Los Angeles to speak at a large conference in the church where I had received the Lord. I had grown up in the things of God there for 23 years before Michael and I were led by God to move to Tennessee. By that time the church had grown to thousands in attendance and was well known globally. For this particular conference, people had come from all over the world. The large sanctuary was full.

I again shared about my past and the damage that was done by being locked in a closet so much of my early childhood. And how everything I did to try and stop the emotional pain I experienced daily only led me closer to death. But God rescued me when I received Jesus as my Savior, and He transformed my life.

At that conference, it was great to see so many of my old friends again. One woman in particular was Rebecca—Pastor Jack's daughter and also one of my dear prayer partners for a few years. I didn't get to talk to her much because of the number of people coming up to say hello, although we did get to have a quick lunch together, along with my daughter, who had traveled with me.

"I have something to tell you that the Lord has shown me. I'll put it in a letter and send it to you," Rebecca said.

Shortly after Mandy and I returned home, I received the promised letter.

In it was the same word from the Lord that the other two women had spoken to me. Only Rebecca's letter was far more detailed, and it was written out so I could read it again and again. Plus, because I knew Rebecca well and for such a long time, I considered her to be very solid in the Word. I knew she heard from God in profound ways, and I trusted her walk with Him completely. After I read what she wrote, I realized God had prepared me to hear this message from her by sending the other two women who had already spoken to me about it in similar words.

This is what she wrote:

> *Dear Stormie,*
>
> I want to share something that I felt the Lord spoke to me when you talked about the closets of your childhood. He said, "Those closets were ordained by My hand to spare Stormie's life. What Satan meant for evil, I have turned for good. Frightening though it was, it became a place of safety where her life was protected and preserved." I was so moved by the Lord's words to my heart, because we both know how He redeems *absolutely everything.*

When I read Rebecca's words, they deeply touched my heart, mind, and spirit. Such a message from the mouth of three witnesses could not be ignored. My eyes were opened like never before. The first two times this was suggested to me, I couldn't see why God would use something so damaging to protect me. I couldn't connect those dots at all. But Rebecca's words about how *God redeems absolutely everything* became clear. Not only had He set me free from my past, but He had redeemed everything to the point that all the painful and damaging things that had happened to me He was using for good.

As I pondered this in depth, I wondered, *How many other blessings in my life have I not seen, or perhaps even resisted, that were designed by God to be a place of safety for me?*

I thought about the move to Tennessee. That certainly had become a place of safety for me and my family from the earthquake. And the hospital specializing in treatment of the precise cancer that threatened my husband's life was there in Nashville. And there was so much more. I consider Nashville a place of safety for us from so many things.

I'm not saying that every bad thing that happens to us is a good thing. But God takes what the enemy intends for evil and turns it around to bring good out of it.

All of my early life was ruled by fear. I was afraid of my mother, afraid of other children, afraid of people, afraid of heights, afraid of the dark, afraid of dying, afraid of car accidents, afraid of going to the hospital, afraid of not getting to the hospital in time, afraid of every possible thing that could happen to me. I had countless fears until a spirit of fear controlled my life.

I read in the Bible where God said, "'For the oppression of the poor, for the sighing of the needy, now I will arise,' says the LORD; 'I will set him in *the safety for which he yearns.*'" [2]

God had put me and my family in a place of safety that I had yearned for—for so many years.

When the stalker was following me, it was the most vulnerable and endangered I had ever felt. Yet God kept me and my family safe. He has kept me safe in whatever place He has led me. *The will of God is a place of safety.* That doesn't mean that nothing bad will ever happen, but even when something bad does happen, I sense God's hand of protection and peace in it.

God's peace and safety are not something I ever want to take for granted. The apostle Paul wrote about the day of the Lord that will come. He said, "For you yourselves know perfectly that the day of the Lord so comes as a thief in the night. For when they say, 'Peace and safety!' then sudden destruction comes upon them, as labor pains upon a pregnant woman. And they shall not escape. But you…are not in darkness, so that this Day should overtake you as a thief." [3]

He goes on to say that we who are children of the light must be watchful and sober. He said we are to be always "putting on *the breastplate of faith and love*, and *as a helmet the hope* of salvation." [4]

The "day of the Lord" is the return of Christ, which will come unexpectedly, just like a thief in the night. But the good news for us who believe in God and have received His Son is that we will not live in darkness about this. We will not be taken by surprise. That's because *we are sons and daughters of the light*. We no longer live in the dark. Because we have Jesus, we have the light of His Holy Spirit in us. We can never be truly in the darkness unless we *choose* to walk away from Him and live separated by our own lack of repentance.

Being watchful means praying without ceasing. We are not to be drunk with our own desires but to be alert to all that God is doing, and what He wants to do *in* and *through* us. We are to be prepared for what is ahead. The hour is too late for us not to be.

Years ago, when I first received the Lord, I read a lot in the Bible and in many Christian books about the end-times. At that time I could not see how some of those things could possibly happen. For example, how can *all people* witness the return of the Lord together? Now it's easy to see that, with technology the way it is and how fast it is advancing, this is definitely possible.

We observe certain countries of the world aligning together against other countries, just as it is foretold in the Bible. Everything that has been prophesied could happen at any time, and we are told to be ready for it. We don't have to live in fear because we are children of His light. We were chosen to be saved by Jesus, and we will live in the ultimate place of safety.

We don't have to live in anxiety about the future when we are walking with God. He will always take us to a place of safety. God can even transform the place where we are into a place of safety when we turn to Him. Or He may lift us *out* of it, or walk us *through* it to the place of safety He has for us. God's place of ultimate safety can be found in trusting Him and staying in His light and His will.

That is what I plan to do. And to help others do the same.

# 27

# Staying in the Light

One of the things I learned while working on television, photo sessions, musicals, personal appearances, and live plays is that you must always make sure you stay in the light. Lighting is everything, and bad lighting can kill you.

The same is true in the spirit realm.

When you receive Jesus, the light of His Spirit is in you, so you always have His light as long as you don't reject it. But if you want all of the benefits—also known as blessings—you must deliberately *stay* in His light. Choosing to walk outside the path God illuminates for you can kill you too.

Not living God's way gets you off that well-lit path.

The truth is, God sees *all* sin. He says, "My eyes are on all their ways; they are not hidden from My face, nor is their iniquity hidden from My eyes." [1]

When we receive Jesus, He forgives all of our sins of the past. That's because He already paid the price for them, which is death. What God then sees in our heart is the perfection, righteousness, and sinlessness of Jesus. It's a remarkable exchange. But from then on, our heart is a tablet upon which the truth about us is written. Our sins are tattooed on our heart permanently, and God sees it all. Unless we repent of them—and God's forgiveness erases them completely—they become a continual reminder that we do not have a repentant heart.

When I first began getting free of my past, I still couldn't see much of a future for myself. I knew I had new life, but I also saw how much damage I had done trying to live life on my own terms—trying to meet my own needs my own way. We are all unaware to some extent of the way God wants us to live. We miss seeing what He has for us.

I didn't want to be ungrateful for all that He had done for me, but one night I wept before Him saying, "Lord, You've given me hope and peace and eternal life, and I am forever grateful. But as far as my life ever amounting to anything, how can that ever be? My life is a mess of broken pieces scattered everywhere, and some of them are missing. How can they ever be put back together again? Is it too late for me?"

God met me where I was that night and said, "I am a Redeemer. I redeem all things. I make all things new. Whatever you've lost, I will restore. It doesn't matter what you've done. It doesn't matter what's happened to you. I can take all your hurt, pain, and scars. I can not only heal them, I can make them count for something."

My tears flowed as if they were endless. *How could God ever accomplish all of that?* I wondered. Yet I believed that all things were possible with God, and I'd seen Him do miracles in my life. His words gave me hope.

That kind of redemption didn't happen overnight. It happened step by step as I learned to walk in the light of the Lord—completely submitted to Him and His ways—and allow Him to take me to places I couldn't get to on my own.

Isn't it wonderful to know that when we look at the pieces of our lives and say, "I've destroyed this marriage." "I've messed up this relationship." "I've damaged this child." "I've ruined my health." "I wasted so many years." "I've made bad choices and terrible decisions." "I've chosen my own way over God's ways." "This was stolen from me." "That was lost to me." "My life is a mess of scattered pieces," that the Lord meets us where we are and says, "I have all of the pieces to your life right here in My hand. If you will look to Me, and follow me, I will put them all together again. And not only that, I will make them all count for something."

That's what He did in my life, and I know He can do it in yours.

This is the vision God gave me regarding this—for you as well as for me. You may see your life today in countless pieces, like old broken glass out in front of a liquor store. But when you completely surrender your life to the Lord, He will take all those pieces of your life and create the most exquisite stained glass window through which His light can shine. His light in you can shine through the pieces of your life to be a beautiful beacon of light to others.

God says about those who love Him, "I know the thoughts that I think toward you, says the LORD, thoughts of *peace* and not of evil, to give you a *future* and a *hope.*"[2]

The Bible says, "Eye has not seen, nor ear heard, nor have entered into the heart of man the things which God has prepared for those who love Him."[3]

God wants us to *know Him* and *trust Him* and *live His way* so He can set us free to be all He created us to be. He wants us to live successfully in Him every day so we can move into all He has for us. When we surrender our will to His, we find His liberty. Totally. Utterly. Completely.

Everything I have comes from God. I owe Him my life. But I didn't just accidentally fall out of darkness one day. I believe we are in it—even if we don't think we are—until we choose to receive the One True Light.

But it doesn't stop there. The darkness will keep trying to infiltrate and penetrate our lives as long as we are on this earth. And not only that, what we allow into our lives affects not only us, but also our children, grandchildren, and great-grandchildren as well.

The Bible says that the sins of the fathers will be visited upon the children up to the third and fourth generation. It says when people wonder why disaster happens to them, tell them it is " 'because your fathers have forsaken Me,' says the LORD; 'they have walked after other gods and have served them and worshiped them, and have forsaken Me and not kept My law.' "[4]

Sins of the parents become generational curses that must be broken. And they can only be broken when we maintain a heart that is pleasing to God—a heart that is filled with the light and life of the Lord.

Over and over in the Old Testament God instructs His people to obey

His commandments because that brings blessings. Not living His way brings curses. [5] I know I don't have it in me to successfully direct my own steps and to know the way I should go, but *He* does. [6]

We can't even rise above our own pride, which is the cause of our spiritual blindness. People who allow pride to reign in their heart don't see the darkness they are in. They do things that are an affront to God and believe there will be no consequences. Jesus said, "He who walks in darkness does not know where he is going." [7] I walked in darkness for 28 years and *thought* I kind of knew where I was going, but I only knew where I *wanted* to go. I had no idea of the plans God had for me.

The problem is, as I have clearly learned, that even when we receive the Lord, we can still choose to follow our own heart and do what *we* want and not listen to Him. How many tragedies would have been avoided if the person involved would have asked God, "Is this Your will for my life?" "Should I be doing this?"

God allows us to go where we are determined to go—even to live outside of His favor—but we aren't protected there and cannot be brought to a place of safety. God takes away His peace and blessings from those who reject Him and are rebellious and unrepentant against Him. Evil falls on people who forsake God and His laws and worship and serve other gods. [8]

We cannot even trust our own heart if we want to stay in the light. The Bible says our "heart is deceitful." [9] We can't trust it. How many of us have fallen in the dark because we followed our heart and not our Lord? God knows the truth about us. He searches our heart so that we can be given blessings or not, according to our ways. [10]

*We can stay in His light by staying in His Word.* Thank You, Lord, that "the entrance of Your words gives light; it gives understanding to the simple." [11] "Your word is a lamp to my feet and a light to my path." [12] Thank You that... "You will light my lamp"...and "enlighten my darkness." [13] You, Lord, are "my light and my salvation; whom shall I fear?" [14]

*We stay out of darkness by walking with God.* "Who walks in darkness and has no light? Let him trust in the name of the LORD and rely upon his God." [15]

I have learned that the enemy of our soul will always try to bring us down, or destroy us, or tempt us back into his dark realm with his lies. So even in the dark times of our lives, we can say, "Do not rejoice over me, my enemy; when I fall, I will arise; when I sit in darkness, the LORD will be a light to me." [16]

We must remember that "*we do not wrestle against flesh and blood*," we struggle "against the rulers of the darkness of this age." [17] But Jesus "has delivered us from the power of darkness." [18] We have to identify what is counterfeit, remembering that our enemy can transform himself "into an angel of light." [19] We must stop giving place to the works of darkness and expose them instead. [20]

Jesus said, "I am the light of the world. He who follows Me shall not walk in darkness, but have the light of life." [21] This is a promise to you and me. But will we turn down the opportunity to follow Him because we don't want to give up the darkness? (Of unforgiveness? Of doubt? Of our idols? Of our own selfish desires?)

We cannot stumble through our life like a dead person. *We have to wake up and see what is happening.* "Awake, you who sleep, arise from the dead, and Christ will give you light." [22] We must make the clear distinction between the darkness of the realm of the enemy of God and our own soul, and the One True Light of God, His Son, and His Spirit—the light in us that never goes out.

I have lived in the darkness and I didn't like it. I praise God for the gift of His light in me. I ask God every day to help me stay in the light of His love, truth, and life.

That is my goal for the rest of my life.

## 28

# Let the Redeemed Say So

The miracle is that I lived.

I always felt there had to be something better for me, but after searching for years for a "better life," I couldn't find it. In fact, every day it all seemed more hopeless than the day before. I certainly never dreamed I had a purpose and God had a plan for me.

I know I couldn't have existed much longer the way things were going. I never thought I would survive beyond my thirties, let alone have a marriage that lasted—with children and grandchildren! I believed those kinds of blessings would never be in the cards for me. I had proven to myself without doubt that my life had an unfathomable dark side, and I believed it could never be overcome, no matter how many ways I tried to do so.

One of the greatest gifts is coming to the point where you know you will not be alive without a miracle from God. The utter dependence of being certain you can do nothing lasting or good without Him—including staying alive—can be liberating.

I looked for light in all the wrong places. I didn't identify or receive the light that never goes out for all eternity, so I carried in me the consequences for everything I did that was against God's ways.

Jesus said He didn't come to judge us, but to save us.[1] But He not only wants to save us *from* something, He wants to save us *for* something. He wants to save us *from* ourselves and our wrong living. But He also wants to save us *for* His purposes and plans to do great things through us. *His greatness* living *in* us is what enables us to do great things for Him. When we surrendered to Him, He makes us ready so He can shine His light through us into the darkness of this world.

As the world grows darker, we must become instruments through which the light of the Lord shines continually brighter. He says, "Arise, shine; for your light has come! And the glory of the LORD is risen upon you."[2]

His Word says, "If you extend your soul to the hungry and satisfy the afflicted soul, then your light shall dawn in the darkness, and your darkness shall be as the noonday."[3]

Jesus instructs us to let others see His light in us. "You are the light of the world. A city that is set on a hill cannot be hidden. Nor do they light a lamp and put it under a basket, but on a lampstand, and it gives light to all who are in the house."[4]

Jesus appeared to Paul to tell him that He was sent to the people "to open their eyes, in order *to turn them from darkness to light, and from the power of Satan to God*."[5] Paul said to the Christians in Rome, "Let us *cast off the works of darkness*, and let us *put on the armor of light*."[6] This is something we have to choose to do every day.

*God's light in and around us is part of God's protection over us.*

We are to comfort and strengthen those who are fearful and weak. We are to "pursue what is good" for everyone. We are to "*rejoice always, pray without ceasing, in everything give thanks, for this is the will of God*." We are to "*not quench the Spirit*." And we are to "*not despise prophecies*." But rather we are to "*test all things; hold fast to what is good*" and we are to "*abstain from every form of evil*."[7]

Jesus said, "I have come as a light into the world, that whoever believes in Me should not abide in darkness."[8] God wants *us* to be His light to those who are in darkness right now. If people had not done that for me, I would still be in darkness today. In fact, I'm sure I would not be alive today. He wants us who know Him to be "a guide to the blind, a light to those who are in darkness."[9]

The Bible says, "You are a chosen generation…His own special people, *that you may proclaim the praises of Him who called you out of darkness into His marvelous light.*" [10] We are all called out of darkness and into His light in order to proclaim God's praise to others.

We are *to love others like He loves us.* Jesus said, "He who says he is in the light, and hates his brother, is in darkness until now. He who loves his brother abides in the light, and there is no cause for stumbling in him." [11] We have to live in the light of His love in order to allow it to shine through us to others.

We cannot do this on our own. Our human love doesn't have what it takes, but God's love in us does. We must receive God's love in all its fullness, we must show our love to God in our worship of Him so He can fill us with more of His love, and that will enable us to love others in a way that pleases Him.

This is the way I have prayed for myself and for others with regard to all that. Make it a prayer for yourself too.

*Lord, I thank You* that You bring light into our dark places. "You are my lamp, O LORD," and You "enlighten my darkness." [12] I don't have to live in fear "of the pestilence that walks in darkness, nor of the destruction that lays waste at noonday." [13] I am grateful that, for the people who love You, we can always find Your light in our dark times. Your Word says that "unto the upright there arises light in the darkness; He is gracious, and full of compassion, and righteous." [14] So even when I am going through a dark time and feel that the enemy is trying to put me back in darkness, I know Your light is always there, shining within me. King David said, "The enemy has persecuted my soul; he has crushed my life to the ground; he has made me dwell in darkness, like those who have long been dead." [15] I have also felt that too, Lord. But now I know that because I walk with You, my future is secure, no matter how it feels at the time.

You have said of those who love and serve You that "the

darkness shall cover the earth, and deep darkness the people," but You will arise over us, and Your glory will be seen upon us. [16] Your Word says, "Woe to those who call evil good, and good evil; who put darkness for light, and light for darkness; who put bitter for sweet, and sweet for bitter!" [17] Help me to make a clear distinction between what is evil and what is good in Your eyes.

I have walked in darkness, and I have seen a great light. I have lived in the land of the shadow of death, until upon me a light has shined. [18] Jesus, You came "to give light to those who sit in darkness and the shadow of death, to guide our feet into the way of peace." [19] Thank You, our "Father of lights, with whom there is no variation or shadow of turning" [20] that You are always at high noon on the sundial, and in You there is no shadow, only light. Thank You, Lord, that my path to the future "is like the shining sun, that shines ever brighter unto the perfect day." [21]

In Jesus' name I pray.

❈

The Bible says, "Let the redeemed of the LORD say so, whom He has redeemed from the hand of the enemy." [22] I have been redeemed from the hand of the enemy and transformed in every way. I am hopefully always becoming more like the Lord, and so I have a daily journey on that path, which will not end until I go to be with Him for eternity.

Because of whose I am, I am called to proclaim who *He is,* and what *He has done* for me.

And so I have.

# Notes

**Chapter 9**
1. John 12:46
2. John 1:4
3. John 1:5
4. Romans 8:9

**Chapter 11**
1. Isaiah 47:13 NIV
2. Deuteronomy 18:10-12
3. Isaiah 40:2
4. Matthew 4:16

**Chapter 12**
1. 2 Timothy 1:7
2. Psalm 63:1 KJV
3. Psalm 51:10
4. See Psalm 90:8
5. John 14:23

**Chapter 13**
1. 2 Timothy 2:5 NIV
2. Deuteronomy 7:26 NIV
3. 1 John 4:18 NIV
4. 1 John 2:5 NIV

**Chapter 14**
1. 2 Corinthians 3:18; Psalm 84:7
2. Psalm 3:18 NIV (emphasis added)
3. 2 Corinthians 3:17
4. Psalm 72:12

**Chapter 22**
1. http://www.caltech-era.org/northridge.htm

**Chapter 23**
1. Psalm 66:18

**Chapter 25**
1. Philippians 4:13

**Chapter 26**
1. 2 Corinthians 13:1
2. Psalm 12:5 (emphasis added)
3. 1 Thessalonians 5:2-4
4. 1 Thessalonians 5:8 (emphasis added)

**Chapter 27**
1. Jeremiah 16:17
2. Jeremiah 29:11 (emphasis added)
3. 1 Corinthians 2:9
4. Jeremiah 16:11
5. See Deuteronomy 28:1-68; Jeremiah 11:3-5
6. See Jeremiah 10:23
7. John 12:35
8. See Jeremiah 16:13 and 17:4
9. Jeremiah 17:9
10. Jeremiah 17:10
11. Psalm 119:130
12. Psalm 119:105
13. Psalm 18:28
14. Psalm 27:1

15. Isaiah 50:10
16. Micah 7:8
17. Ephesians 6:12 (emphasis added)
18. Colossians 1:13
19. 2 Corinthians 11:14
20. See Ephesians 5:11
21. John 8:12
22. Ephesians 5:14

### Chapter 28
1. John 12:47
2. Isaiah 60:1
3. Isaiah 58:10
4. Matthew 5:14-15
5. Acts 26:18 (emphasis added)
6. Romans 13:12 (emphasis added)
7. 1 Thessalonians 5:14-22 (emphasis added)
8. John 12:46
9. Romans 2:19
10. 1 Peter 2:9 (emphasis added)
11. 1 John 2:9-10
12. 2 Samuel 22:29
13. Psalm 91:6
14. Psalm 112:4
15. Psalm 143:3
16. Isaiah 60:2
17. Isaiah 5:20
18. See Isaiah 9:2
19. Luke 1:79
20. James 1:17
21. Proverbs 4:18
22. Psalm 107:2

To learn more about Harvest House books and
to read sample chapters, visit our website:

**www.harvesthousepublishers.com**

HARVEST HOUSE PUBLISHERS
EUGENE, OREGON